# Who's Minding the Story?

*Love + blessings!*
*Jeff Sexton*
*Oct. 2018*

# Who's Minding the Story?

The United Church of Canada Meets *A Secular Age*

Jeff Seaton

FOREWORD BY
Will Willimon

☙PICKWICK *Publications* • Eugene, Oregon

WHO'S MINDING THE STORY?
The United Church of Canada Meets *A Secular Age*

Copyright © 2018 Jeff Seaton. All rights reserved. Except for brief quotations in critical publications or reviews, no part of this book may be reproduced in any manner without prior written permission from the publisher. Write: Permissions, Wipf and Stock Publishers, 199 W. 8th Ave., Suite 3, Eugene, OR 97401.

Pickwick Publications
An Imprint of Wipf and Stock Publishers
199 W. 8th Ave., Suite 3
Eugene, OR 97401

www.wipfandstock.com

PAPERBACK ISBN: 978-1-5326-4245-6
HARDCOVER ISBN: 978-1-5326-4246-3
EBOOK ISBN: 978-1-5326-4247-0

*Cataloguing-in-Publication data:*

Names: Seaton, Jeff

Title: Who's minding the story? : the United Church of Canada meets *A Secular Age* / by Jeff Seaton

Description: Eugene, OR: Pickwick Publications, 2018 | Includes bibliographical references and index.

Identifiers: ISBN 978-1-5326-4245-6 (paperback) | ISBN 978-1-5326-4246-3 (hardcover) | ISBN 978-1-5326-4247-0 (ebook)

Subjects: LCSH: United Church of Canada. | Secularism—Canada.

Classification: LCC BX9881 S33 2018 (print) | LCC BX9881 (ebook)

Scripture quotations are from New Revised Standard Version Bible, copyright © 1989 National Council of the Churches of Christ in the United States of America. Used by permission. All rights reserved.

Manufactured in the U.S.A.                                    07/16/18

This book is dedicated to the people of
the United Church of Canada:

who created a place for me to exercise my gifts
for ministry as a gay man;

who fought for my right to marry my same-sex partner,
and celebrated our wedding;

and who have generously nurtured my gifts, and
forgiven my faults, over the past eighteen years;

and to my husband Don,
whose unfailing love and support
has taught me so much about the love of God.

# Contents

*Foreword by Will Willimon* | ix
*Acknowledgments* | xii
*Introduction* | xiii

## Chapter 1. A Story of "the Sixties" | 1

1.1 A Decade of Ferment 2
1.2 Secular Theology to the Rescue? 5
1.3 A Critique of the Critics 13
1.4 The United Church Responds 14
1.5 Conclusion 16

## Chapter 2. Charles Taylor's Secularization Story | 19

2.1 The "Story" of Secularity 3 20
2.2 The Process of Reform and the Construction of the Immanent Frame 22
2.3 From Mobilization to Authenticity 25
2.4 Where We Live Now—The Age of Authenticity 28
2.5 Excursus: The Gospel According to Charles Taylor 31
2.6 Summary—"A Secular Age" and Our Contemporary Dilemma 32
2.7 Conclusion 35

## Chapter 3. Embracing the Culture's Stories | 37

3.1 Fishing Tips: The Hillhurst Story 39
3.2 Excursus: "The Age of the Spirit" 44
3.3 "Charles Taylor, Meet John Pentland" 47
3.4 Conclusion 56

CONTENTS

## Chapter 4. Writing God Out of the Story | 58

    4.1 Without God  60

    4.2 A Post-Theistic Church  68

    4.3 Transcendence, Immanence, and "Transimmanence"  72

    4.4 Charles Taylor in Dialogue with Gretta Vosper  73

    4.5 Conclusion  77

## Chapter 5. Finding the Heart of the Story | 79

    5.1 The Pews Are Still Too Comfortable  81

    5.2 Beyond the Lowest Common Denominator  84

    5.3 Growing Up and the Quest  88

    5.4 Church and Culture  93

    5.5 Conclusion: Returning to the Heart of the Story  99

## Chapter 6. The Next Chapter of the Story | 101

    6.1 Two Visions of the Future  102

    6.2 "Secular Church": A Vision of Continuity  103

    6.3 A Divided Church?  108

    6.4 "Progressive Orthodoxy": A Vision of Renewal  111

    6.5 Getting From Here to There  117

    6.6 Conclusion  122

## Conclusion | 124

*Author Biography* | 127

*Bibliography* | 129

# Foreword

SOME YEARS AGO I participated in an extensive sociological study of trends in mainline Protestantism in the US. We were just beginning to notice that liberal, mainline Protestantism was in trouble. The only specific insight that I remember from the study was theological: mainline, liberal, American Christianity is in trouble because our clergy have given people a theological rationale for godlessness. This theological critique came from sociologists!

While we were sleeping, without intending to do so, we gave people the intellectual ammunition they needed to steer clear of the church and its claims in order to descend more deeply into their subjective selves. Personal experience with a wide array of churches in the intervening years has confirmed the validity of this thesis. Liberal Christianity in North America is in free fall for lots of reasons—low birthrates, a graying membership, our churches stuck in areas of declining population, we failed to reach the waves of new arrivals from other cultures, and a host of sociological, anthropological factors. However, a more important element in our demise may be theological.

We failed to keep our eye on the ball, to keep the main thing, the main thing, to take care of business, to mind the store. I could pile on a few more tropes, but I'll let Jeff Seaton put forth the most apt metaphor: *Who's Minding the Story?*

Read Jeff's book and you will see how we have sold our Christian birthright for a mess of pottage (Gen 27), thrown the baby out with the bathwater, sold the farm. *Enough!* (What is there about a crisis that provokes metaphorical overload in us preachers?)

For some decades now, those of us coming over the Canadian/American border have suspected that the mainline Canadian church could be the bellwether, the canary in the mine, the . . . *stop!* The disestablishment and disenfranchisement of liberal, Protestant Christianity has been more apparent in Canadian churches than in churches I have served south of the border. For us Americans, the Canadian Christian situation is not only disturbing but also an important warning.

After a service in a mostly empty United Church in the Canadian west, the pastor and I sat gloomily in his study and he, sensing my depression, shook his finger at me declaring, "Just you wait! Your day is coming. You shall be as we."

That pastor, though a terrible host, was prescient in his predictions. The line between a shrinking United Church and my dwindling United Methodist Church is thin.

Jeff has given us a straight-talking, revealing book that puts its finger on our wound—our flaccid, vague Christology has robbed liberal Christianity of anything to say to the world that the world cannot obtain more easily without all the baggage incurred by claiming that a Jew from Nazareth who lived briefly, died violently, and rose unexpectedly is the truth about God. Thousands of Canadians seem to be saying, "If it's not about Jesus, why bother?"

Building upon the thought of fellow Canadian Charles Taylor, Jeff illuminates our situation. We liberals put our money on the wrong horse, backed the wrong player. *Stop!* We are paying dearly for our intellectual mistakes. Democratic, subjective, vague liberalism has proven to be an inadequate means of thinking about the thick, demanding, odd story that is the gospel of Christ.

Jeff takes aim at specific exemplars of the theological failure of mainline Christianity in Canada, showing how in leaning over to speak to the world they fell in face down, failing to say anything to the world that the world doesn't already know. He puts some popular preachers in conversation with Charles Taylor and comes forth with some troubling insights. Surprise, Gretta Vosper is but the tip of the iceberg. *Enough!*

Jeff demonstrates how the oddness and peculiarity of the Christian story does not easily translate into the stories that the world tells itself. Little about the gospel is innate or available to modern people without the substance and agency of Christ.

I hasten to add that Jeff's is a very helpful, hopeful book. Jeff is not only a seasoned pastor who writes from the trenches but also a member of a new generation who sees the intellectual, theological challenges ahead of us in a way that is different from us old guys.

FOREWORD

Reading Jeff's book gave me hope for the future and provided a way of recommitting myself to the distinctive, odd, wonderful story of Jesus Christ, reconciling God's world to God.

Will Willimon

Professor of Christian Ministry
Duke Divinity School, Durham NC
United Methodist Bishop, retired

# Acknowledgments

This book would not have come to completion without the kindness, encouragement, and support of three gifted teachers: William Willimon, who served as my thesis supervisor in the Doctor of Ministry program at Duke Divinity School; Phyllis Airhart of Emmanuel College at the University of Toronto, who served as second reader for my thesis; and Craig Hill, former Director of the Doctor of Ministry Program at Duke and now Dean of Perkins School of Theology. Craig welcomed our cohort into the Doctor of Ministry program and modeled the Christian virtues of humility, generosity, and hospitality throughout our five terms of course work. Phyllis, a United Church of Canada historian, provided key inspiration through her recent magisterial history of the denomination, and through her keen United Church and Canadian eye applied to the various drafts of this document. Will served as a source of inspiration and as a wise mentor and guide, offering the insights of his keen and broad intellect throughout. For all of the ways each of them contributed to improving my work in these pages, I offer my thanks. To all three, for their scholarship, their faith, and their friendship, I remain deeply grateful.

I also want to express my deep gratitude to the people of Trinity United Church in Vernon, British Columbia, for their support, encouragement, and patience through this journey, and especially over the months of my sabbatical. Finally, to my husband Don, and to our family, thank you for standing by me in the moments of frustration and the moments of joy, as the journey toward fulfillment of this dream unfolded over the past few years. Your generous love makes all the difference in my life.

# Introduction

Evidently there was an intellectual world, a world of culture and grace, of lofty thoughts and the inspiring communion of real knowledge, where creeds were not of importance, and where men asked one another, not "Is your soul saved?" but "Is your mind well furnished?" Theron had the sensation of having been invited to become a citizen of this world. The thought so dazzled him that his impulses were dragging him forward to take the new oath of allegiance before he had time to reflect upon what it was he was abandoning.[1]

HAROLD FREDERIC'S 1896 NOVEL *The Damnation of Theron Ware* can be read as a parable of the liberal mainline Protestant church's encounter with modernity and secularization. When we first meet the protagonist at the beginning at the novel, Theron Ware is presented as being amongst the best of his kind: a young, gifted, small-town Methodist parson with a simple and innocent faith that sustains his vocation and underpins his domestic life. As the tale unfolds, we witness Theron's perverse "progress" from this guileless and reasonably contented state as he encounters three characters who symbolize the forces with which the church has contended in the modern period. First, there is Father Forbes, the older Catholic priest, whose worldliness and erudition reveal his deep immersion in the historical-critical method of biblical scholarship. He shocks Theron with his reference to "this Christ-myth of ours."[2] Then there is Celia Madden, a rich, young, beautiful, and free-spirited woman who declares herself a devotee of Greek philosophy and culture. Finally, there is Dr. Ledsmar, a scientist whose cruelty and inhumanity are revealed by the experiments he conducts upon his manservant.

1. Frederic, *Damnation of Theron Ware*, 132.
2. Frederic, *Damnation of Theron Ware*, 71.

INTRODUCTION

Critical scholarship, the allure of art, beauty, and uninhibited sexuality, and modern science: these three together open up previously unimagined vistas for the young pastor, and he is at once ashamed of his simple, traditional faith, and the life he has constructed around it.

Frederic's preferred title for the work—and the title under which it was published in Great Britain—was *Illumination*, an ironic reference to the dawning light of reason spread abroad by the new Darwinian science, by historical critical scholarship, and by the philosophical and cultural currents of the Enlightenment: an illumination that dispelled and dispersed the gloom of religion and its ghosts. It is an ironic title because of course Theron's illumination is anything but; it is rather a descent into darkness. Theron grows increasingly confused, flailing about, grasping after the gifts he believes the others possess while the simple light of faith that once illumined his life grows increasingly dim. The more he chases after what the others have, the more they recoil from him in disgust. What inspired them to draw him into their circle in the first place was his innocence and simplicity, his simple faith that seemed so different from their worldly cynicism: "It was like the smell of early spring in the country to come in contact with you."[3] But Theron despised the gift he carried, seeing it instead as an embarrassment to be got rid of, so that he might prove acceptable to his new friends. He was so determined to be seen as modern, sophisticated, and grown up that he despised his birthright and ends up hollow and broken.

The mainline Protestant church in the modern era knows the powerful allure of each of the forces with which the Rev. Theron Ware had to contend. For well over a century science seems to have won every argument with religion, leaving God with ever diminishing grounds for existence. The philosophical ideals of the Enlightenment, and the artistic and aesthetic ideals of the Romantic period, have contributed to the creation of alternative sources of meaning more enticing than the sterility of the church's fusty traditions. Historical-critical scholarship has undercut the central meaning of the church's story, revealing its treasure as just so much illusion that we have finally outgrown as we have come of age. Like Theron Ware, the liberal mainline church has at times responded to modernity by reevaluating itself in light of its new potential friends and finding itself wanting. The church's critics, both from within and from outside, have contributed to this call for reevaluation, inviting the church to "get with the times," to get on board with the changes wrought by modernity.

3. Frederic, *Damnation of Theron Ware*, 321–22.

INTRODUCTION

For liberal mainline Protestant churches like the United Church of Canada, this call grew increasingly loud and incessant in the 1960s:

> The sixties marked a pivotal point in Western culture and saw the blossoming of a deepened sense of human autonomy and freedom, ranging from militant peace movements to the triumph of rock music to sexual liberation to celebrations of the "secular city." Theologically, Bonhoeffer's provocative but ambiguous phrases about a human "coming of age" and a "religionless Christianity" were taken up and understood . . . as adumbrations of the end of Christian theism, if not of the death of God.[4]

This book seeks to explore the phenomena of the United Church of Canada's response to these trends, beginning with an account of the denomination's tumultuous journey through this pivotal decade. I will argue that the secular theology that emerged in the 1960s—with its particular response to the scientific revolution, to historical criticism of Scripture, and to the philosophical and cultural currents of the modern era—became highly influential in determining the trajectory of the United Church over the ensuing decades. I will show that two contemporary proposals for the future development of the United Church—that of the Rev. Dr. John Pentland of Hillhurst United Church in Calgary and that of the Rev. Gretta Vosper of West Hill United Church in Toronto—can trace their lineage back to the emergence of secular theology in the denomination in the 1960s.

Mindful of the parable of Theron Ware, however, this book will also explore the question of the costs of the United Church's response to modernity and secularization over the past half century. What if the account of secularization upon which secular theology has been built is in some ways flawed? What would that mean for approaches and proposals that incorporate secular theology's read of history? Canadian philosopher Charles Taylor, in his recent work *A Secular Age*, offers an account of secularization significantly at odds with the standard narrative.[5] This book will use Taylor's work as the basis for a critical analysis of the approaches of Pentland and Vosper as part of a broader discussion of the trends within the United Church since the 1960s. I will show that Taylor's critique significantly weakens the foundations of the arguments advanced by secularists and calls into question significant aspects of proposals based on these arguments. I will argue that attempts to accommodate cultural trends over the

---

4. Wyatt, "New Atheism," 24.
5. Taylor, *Secular Age*.

INTRODUCTION

past fifty years have caused the United Church of Canada to give up too much. Like Theron Ware, the United Church of Canada has been tempted to place a higher value on the gifts others seem to possess than on its own treasures. The book will conclude with a call for the United Church to work at recovering a stronger connection to its heritage as the best means for it to be of service in the world.

Taylor presents his account of secularization as a story, rather than as a purely analytical argument, believing that the stories we tell about historical developments are enormously influential. The structure of this book is inspired by Taylor's approach, and will focus on the ways the story of secularization has been told, and continues to be told, in the United Church of Canada. Taylor notes that doing justice to his project of describing secularization in the Christian West in the modern era would require something beyond the scope of his 900-page tome, and offers this caveat:

> I ask the reader who picks up this book not to think of it as a continuous story-and-argument, but rather as a set of interlocking essays, which shed light on each other. I hope the general thrust of my thesis will emerge from this sketchy treatment, and will suggest to others further ways of developing, applying, modifying, and transposing the argument.[6]

I offer a similar caveat: doing justice to the attempt to describe responses to secularization in the United Church of Canada since the 1960s is a project that would extend much beyond the bounds of this volume. The past half century has been a period of accelerated social and cultural change with many forces impacting the trajectories of mainline Protestant denominations. The United Church of Canada is also an incredibly diverse institution which embraces a variety of theological perspectives as well as significant regional variation. Furthermore, as Taylor's argument demonstrates, any talk of secularization inevitably invites a quest further back in history, and a fuller treatment of the questions raised in this discussion would need to engage the Fundamentalist-Modernist controversy in the early twentieth century, the debates over science in the nineteenth century, the Enlightenment, and the various cultural forces at play all the way back to the period of Reform with which Taylor begins his story. Or the conversation could be pushed even further back into history, as the church since its inception has wrestled with the issues of its relationship to the "secular" world.

6. Taylor, *Secular Age*, ix.

INTRODUCTION

So, some limits need to be set. I am of necessity telling a partial story. I choose to focus on the period since the 1960s, since it is within the living memory of most of those who currently participate in the life of the United Church of Canada. I do so recognizing that the 1960s was not the ultimate origin point of the set of themes that will be discussed in these pages, but that it was a time in which these themes were crystallized in a particular way that has remained influential in the denomination ever since. In other words, the 1960s set the terms and some of the key language in which the conversation continues to be engaged. I also choose to focus on two particular manifestations of United Church ecclesiology—those of Pentland and Vosper—in the belief that these approaches are highly influential in the denomination today. The evidence I see for the influence of these two approaches is based on a variety of sources: the attention paid to them by official bodies of the denomination; the attention paid to them by unofficial organs such as *The United Church Observer*, the independent denominational magazine, as well as by mainstream media in Canada; and the anecdotal evidence of conversations throughout the church and on social media platforms. Finally, I tell the story from my particular personal perspective, as a person born in 1964, ordained to ministry in the United Church of Canada in 2007, and having served large urban, rural, and small town congregations in British Columbia over the past decade. I share Taylor's hope that "the general thrust of my thesis will emerge from this sketchy treatment, and will suggest to others further ways of developing, applying, modifying, and transposing the argument." I offer this book as an entry point to a conversation that I believe our denomination needs to have. I am less interested in being proved right about any particular point in my argument than I am in encouraging reflection on our denomination's recent history, on our choices and trajectory, and on our relationship to the story at the heart of our faith.

The argument will proceed as follows: chapter 1 will provide a brief overview of the changes the 1960s brought to the United Church of Canada; chapter 2 will provide a summary of the argument presented by Taylor in *A Secular Age* and will conclude with a set of four themes that will be used in the analytical chapters that follow; chapters 3 and 4 will consider, respectively, the proposals of John Pentland and Gretta Vosper, using the analysis based on the themes from Taylor; chapter 5 will summarize the argument and advocate the recovery of a robust connection to Christian tradition; finally, drawing on the evidence provided, chapter 6 will outline two visions for the future of the denomination.

# Chapter 1. A Story of "the Sixties"

The Church must get with the world, or it will surely perish.

—Pierre Berton, *The Comfortable Pew*[1]

WITHOUT QUESTION, THE 1960s was a pivotal decade in the history of the United Church of Canada: important denominational leadership positions saw generational change; a home-grown Christian education program called the New Curriculum was launched to great acclaim and great controversy; and official bodies within the denomination called for a wholesale reorientation of the church's resources, embracing a stance of "listening to the world." These changes in the denomination took place within, and were responses to, wider social, cultural, and theological forces that strongly affected mainline Protestantism in Canada during the decade.

This chapter will begin with a historical overview of some of the social and cultural factors in the wider Canadian context that impacted mainline Protestantism. I will then examine some of the main changes that occurred within the denomination in the 1960s, before turning to an examination of the theological currents that had the greatest influence on the mainline churches. In the middle of the decade, both the Anglican Church and the United Church invited prominent outsiders to pen critiques of their respective denominations. These critiques and other works of the time offered diagnoses of the problems facing mainline Protestantism and outlined prescriptions for significant change. I will present a summary of these critiques and prescriptions to provide a sense of how the United Church was seen by many of its critics, its leaders, and its participants during this pivotal decade. This framework understanding of the problems identified and the solutions proposed during this decade will be important as we examine the subsequent development of the United Church.

1. Berton, *Comfortable Pew*, 27.

## 1.1 A Decade of Ferment

As it was in many North Atlantic societies, the 1960s in Canada was a decade of ferment.[2] Commemoration of the country's centennial in 1967 marked the capstone of a decade in which Canada transitioned from its historic colonial identity to a more confident, pluralist, and multicultural self-image. At the start of the decade, however, the massive changes that were to sweep through society, culture, and religious life in Canada went largely unnoticed. Throughout the 1950s a postwar hungering for normalcy had boosted church participation; in 1961, fully 94 percent of Canadians claimed affiliation with a Christian church.[3] Gary Miedema describes the Canada of this era as stable and staid in appearance, marked by the enduring influence of a relatively small group of Anglo-Protestant and French Roman Catholic elites who made up the leadership ranks of both the churches and state institutions.[4]

Despite such appearances, processes were already underway that would irrevocably alter this image of Canada. Postwar immigration patterns created a more ethnically diverse population; economic prosperity generated demands for social and political reform; and the expansion of the state into areas that were once considered part of the church's domain—education, health care, and social welfare—presented a significant challenge to the existing order.[5] Added to these social and cultural pressures was the key political issue that would dominate Canadian national life for decades to come—the issue of national unity. The Quiet Revolution launched by the government of Québec beginning in 1960 signaled a major challenge to the old order, raising the possibility that one of Canada's most populous regions might secede from Confederation. In response, "when the Liberal Party under Pearson took back the reins of government from the Conservatives in 1963, it responded to an increasingly diverse and demanding population and to the themes of participatory democracy and equality, not by maintaining a British and Christian Canada, but by dismantling its parts."[6] This was seen as necessary in order to make way for

---

2. "A Decade of Ferment" is the title of John Webster Grant's discussion of the 1960s in his volume *The Church in the Canadian Era*, 184–206.
3. Miedema, *For Canada's Sake*, 16.
4. Miedema, *For Canada's Sake*, 18.
5. Miedema, *For Canada's Sake*, 25–31.
6. Miedema, *For Canada's Sake*, 45.

## CHAPTER 1. A STORY OF "THE SIXTIES"

new national symbols of Canada that would transcend the particularities of race, language, and cultural heritage.

In the quest for national unity and a more inclusive vision of what it meant to be Canadian, religious particularity was also seen as an impediment. As the federal government prepared for celebrations of Canada's centennial year in 1967, it created the Canadian Interfaith Conference (CIC) to support the involvement of religious communities in Centennial celebrations. The CIC "was an attempt to draw on a lowest common religious denominator—one that emphasized such state-friendly ideals as loyalty, love of neighbour, and generosity of spirit—in order to stabilize and legitimize the Canadian nation."[7] It would be difficult to overstate the impact of the national unity question on the Canadian psyche in the post-1960 period. Perhaps the strong links forged in the 1960s between the interests of national unity and the importance of "lowest common denominator" religion have contributed to a mindset amongst mainline Protestants that values faith expressions that are invisible, indistinguishable from the markers of good citizenship.

As with the country as a whole, so it was for the United Church of Canada as a denomination.[8] At the dawn of the 1960s, the United Church of Canada was still a relatively young church, having been founded in 1925 as an organic union of Methodists, Congregationalists, and most Presbyterians in Canada. At first glance all seemed well, though troubling signs were beginning to appear: "membership was still on the upswing.... Fundraising had set a new record, ministers's salaries were up, and properties were in good shape. However, other numbers were not so reassuring: funerals were up, while baptisms, confirmations, and adult professions of faith were down."[9] And, like the country as a whole, the denomination was on the cusp of major institutional change. For the first four decades of its life, its leaders had been drawn from members of the founding generation, but "by the mid-1960s only two of the national church officers had been ordained before 1925."[10]

---

7. Miedema, *For Canada's Sake*, 77. Note on spelling: where this book cites Canadian sources, the original Canadian spelling of words is maintained.

8. For a comprehensive overview of the United Church during this period, see Airhart, *Church with the Soul of a Nation*. For a study focused on issues related to the New Curriculum and the dialogue between theological liberalism and evangelicalism in the 1960s United Church, see Flatt, *After Evangelicalism*.

9. Airhart, *Church with the Soul of a Nation*, 225.

10. Airhart, *Church with the Soul of a Nation*, 226.

One of the more consequential leadership transitions of this period was the accession of J. Raymond Hord to the office of Secretary of the Board of Evangelism and Social Service (E&SS), replacing James R. Mutchmor who had served in this role for the previous 26 years. Unusually amongst Protestant churches, the United Church had chosen to hold together under one board functions that were often separated: the work of evangelism and of social outreach.[11] Under Hord's stewardship, the social outreach work of E&SS came to the fore, with evangelism—rechristened as "new evangelism"—reinterpreted in a social justice key: "'Evangelism is not church extension,' (buildings) he said. Nor is it 'conversion in a narrow, individualistic, stereotyped sense.' Nor is it proselytism. Rather, it was about working out one's salvation in one's daily life and work."[12] Hord was strongly influenced by Harvey Cox's "secular city" theology and its call to get out of the church and into the world: "Jesus is calling us to get out of our church structures and formal organisations to stand with the people who most need our help—the alcoholic, the addict, the unemployed, the divorcee, the deserted, the school drop-out, the poor, the mentally ill, in order that we may bring them hope."[13] Hord's call for the United Church to "listen to the world" was not without its critics. Evangelicals within the church questioned what seemed like an overtly political turn in the priorities identified by E&SS.[14]

By the mid-1960s a growing divide between evangelicals and liberals in the United Church was becoming apparent. If the "new evangelism" raised questions about their church's direction for evangelicals, the New Curriculum was the clearest sign of fundamentally different understandings of theology at the heart of the denomination. Conceived in the early 1950s (and inspired by a curriculum launched by the Presbyterian Church in the United States in 1948), the New Curriculum went through a lengthy period of gestation before its launch in 1964. Phyllis D. Airhart argues that the delays that beset its development—particularly in the context of a rapidly changing cultural milieu—ensured that it "appealed to neither conservative evangelicals nor a younger generation of more radical liberals."[15] Kevin N. Flatt, in a book that focuses on the New Curriculum and the 1960s

---

11. Airhart, *Church with the Soul of a Nation*, 229.
12. Beardsall, "Ray Hord," 53.
13. Board of Evangelism and Social Service, *Listen*, 8.
14. Airhart, *Church with the Soul of a Nation*, 239–40.
15. Airhart, *Church with the Soul of a Nation*, 171.

in the United Church, goes further, suggesting that "the curriculum soon became the centre of a major controversy that rocked the United Church and played no small part in permanently altering the direction and identity of the denomination."[16] While the historical record is clear as to the controversy surrounding the introduction of the New Curriculum,[17] it is difficult to assess the validity of Flatt's wider claim as to its impact on the direction and identity of the denomination. Given the wider social, political, cultural, and theological currents of the 1960s, there are simply too many variables involved to be able to isolate the impact of the curriculum. Flatt acknowledges that the controversy over the curriculum brought to light long-existing patterns in the denomination:

> The ensuing conflict publicly established that the bulk of United Church leaders and ministers were strenuously opposed to evangelical views, and in some cases actually regarded evangelicalism with undisguised contempt. It put a spotlight on the division between evangelicals and modernists (a division that had been obscured by past practices) and showed that the church establishment was located firmly in the modernist camp. In this respect the controversy did not so much *create* an evangelical-modernist divide, as *reveal* it in a public and unavoidable way.[18]

At the heart of Flatt's argument is the assertion that there remained, into the 1960s, a profound gulf between the theology of clergy and church leaders on the one hand, and that of the people in the pews. While modernist biblical scholarship had been taught in Canadian seminaries since the late nineteenth century, its insights "did come as a shock—whether a welcome revelation or an affront—to many churchgoers in 1964."[19]

## 1.2 Secular Theology to the Rescue?

This notion of a gulf between the pulpit and the pew was central to a series of highly controversial—and, in some cases, hugely popular—books that were published in the early to mid-1960s. First out of the gate was *Honest to God* by John A. T. Robinson, Bishop of Woolwich, a runaway

16. Flatt, *After Evangelicalism*, 104.
17. See Flatt, *After Evangelicalism*, 104–43, and Grant, *Church in the Canadian Era*, 186–87; for a more nuanced view, see Airhart, *Church with the Soul of a Nation*, 264–67.
18. Flatt, *After Evangelicalism*, 142.
19. Flatt, *After Evangelicalism*, 116.

bestseller when it was published in 1963.[20] According to the appraisal of an admirer, "Robinson says that twentieth-century man can no longer be treated as a child who needs to believe in charming fairy tales in order to understand eternal truths."[21] Other books which followed in the genre of secular theology also emphasized the idea of growing up, reaching adulthood, and throwing off the tutelage of a childish faith. Cox, in *The Secular City*, notes that the process of secularization "suggests . . . a whole range of images—growing up, assuming the responsibilities of an heir, executing an accountable stewardship—which appear throughout the New Testament."[22] These are fitting images for a decade of ferment, as all of the old, established markers of identity and authority come under pressure from new arrivals on the scene.

In Canada, the Anglican church commissioned well-known author and journalist Pierre Berton "to examine the church as critically as he wished from the viewpoint of an outsider."[23] The result was published as *The Comfortable Pew* in 1965 and it quickly became the bestselling book published in Canada to that time. The United Church immediately followed suit with *Why the Sea Is Boiling Hot*, a collection of critical essays by Berton and five other leading Canadian journalists; the collection was rounded off by four essays written by an editorial team of the Board of Evangelism and Social Service. The following year saw the publication of *The Restless Church*, yet another collection of essays written in response to *The Comfortable Pew*, featuring contributions both supportive and critical of that earlier work. Taken together, these three Canadian publications offered a brutally frank and unsparing assessment of the state of mainline Protestantism in Canada in the 1960s.

While these three books focused on the specific ills of Canadian mainline churches, their critiques were informed by the secular theology popularized by Robinson and Cox. In order to analyze and summarize the critiques presented in the three Canadian works, I will employ a typology presented by Cox in *The Secular City*. He describes the function of the church as the continuation of Jesus' ministry as exemplified in Luke 4:18–19: "the church has a threefold responsibility. Theologians call it *kerygma*

20. Robinson, *Honest to God*.

21. Berton, *Comfortable Pew*, 106. Note: this section cites sources written in the 1960s, and thus the language is, to contemporary ears, embarrassingly non-gender-inclusive.

22. Cox, *Secular City*, 130.

23. Berton, *Comfortable Pew*, vii.

(proclamation), *diakonia* (reconciliation, healing, and other forms of service), and *koinonia* (demonstration of the character of the new society)."[24] Of the kerygmatic function, Cox further states that "This broadcasting function of the church is crucial. It makes the church different from any other avant-garde. It has no plan for rebuilding the world. It has only the signal to flash that the One who frees slaves and summons men to maturity is still in business," and "the kerygma itself is articulated only when a man knows that he really is free from dependence on the fates and recognizes that his life is now being placed in his own hands."[25] The *kerygma* is a signal to secular humanity to stand up, to take responsibility, to engage *this* world as a co-creator with God.

The second major function of the church, *diakonia*, is described as "the act of healing and reconciling, binding up wounds and bridging chasms, restoring health to the organism."[26] Noting that efforts at *diakonia* are context-dependent, specific responses to particular social cleavages, Cox suggests some of those that are salient to North American urban contexts in the 1960s: inner city vs. suburbs; issues of economic inequality; racial and ethnic tension; and partisan political divisions.[27] Finally, *koinonia* indicates "that aspect of the church's responsibility in the city which calls for a visible demonstration of what the church is saying in its kerygma and pointing to in its diakonia"; the church expresses its *koinonia* function by "allowing its own life to be shaped by the future Kingdom (not past tradition) and by indicating with its lips and its life where other signs of the Kingdom are appearing."[28] The church that lives out its *koinonia* is marked by provisionality, a willingness to be converted out of structures and forms imported from the surrounding culture and into forms suggested by the countercultural demands of the in-breaking kingdom of God.[29]

The critics who contributed to *The Comfortable Pew*, *Why the Sea Is Boiling Hot*, and *The Restless Church* found the Canadian mainline church of the 1960s wanting in all three of these areas of responsibility. The

24. Cox, *Secular City*, 150.
25. Cox, *Secular City*, 151, 154.
26. Cox, *Secular City*, 157.
27. Cox, *Secular City*, 158.
28. Cox, *Secular City*, 171, 174.

29. Absent from Cox's list are two other widely cited additional functions of the church: *liturgia* (worship and the sacraments) and *didache* (training in the Way of Christ). See, for example, the website for the University Hill Congregation of the United Church of Canada, http://www.uhill.net/teaching.htm.

word-image "the comfortable pew" has had an enduring place in the Canadian ecclesiastical lexicon since the publication of Berton's book in 1965. The phrase neatly summarizes the critique raised by the advocates of secular theology in the Anglican and United churches. Most directly, "the comfortable pew" suggests the ways that mainline Protestantism was failing in its function of *koinonia*. The comfortable mainline church was embedded in its culture; it was an embodiment of (largely) white, suburban, middle-class, affluent, heteronormative society. Berton summarizes:

> The state of tension which should exist between the Church and society, the divine discontent, which is peculiarly Christian, has somehow been lost by an institution which has turned in upon itself, which has become so preoccupied with the status symbols of new edifices, the numbers game of Sunday attendance, the comfortable club atmosphere of the local parish, and above all the need to be safe in order to be successful, that it cannot face the discomforts and sacrifices endured by the prophets of old.[30]

June Callwood offers a scathing description of the church's failure to express *koinonia*, noting that a typical United Church congregation "presents a curious sight, like a busy and slightly boring luxury cruise ship, whose passengers are absorbed by status and self-interest while the ocean around them is thick with numb humanity hopelessly clinging to drowning wreckage."[31] A luxury cruise ship whose passengers are so self-absorbed that they can afford to be bored while their fellows drown is indeed about the furthest thing imaginable from the kingdom of God. Another manifestation of the church's mutation into a country club or cruise ship is the limitations set around the clergy. In an era when clergy were overwhelmingly male, the ideal cleric was "an organization man," committed to meeting the needs of those who paid the bills: "if he can balance a budget, expand facilities, and act as a good executive while developing the relatively innocuous skills of the pulpit—all without stirring up the natives unduly—then he will be counted a success."[32] The emphasis of such "innocuous" preaching should be on helping congregants cultivate the habits of "Peace of Mind and Positive Thinking" so prized in the secular culture.[33]

---

30. Board of Evangelism and Social Service, *Why the Sea*, 2.
31. Board of Evangelism and Social Service, *Why the Sea*, 19.
32. Berton, *Comfortable Pew*, 59.
33. Berton, *Comfortable Pew*, 82.

The antidote to such a failure of *koinonia*, according to the church's secularist critics, lay in a renewed engagement with the world, a renewal of the church's commitment to *diakonia*. For a church that had become inbred and insular, embedded in middle-class culture and its values and insulated from the world, the answer was to recognize "the fundamental Christian teaching that God loves his world and gave his Son for it, to become one of us, to become indeed the friend and companion of those men called 'sinners,' the social outcasts of the day."[34] Echoing Cox's suggestions in *The Secular City*, Berton named a variety of social cleavages to which the church might attend in a ministry of healing and reconciliation: international conflict, in particular the threat of nuclear war; race issues, including the church's paternalistic attitude towards First Nations peoples, and its silence in the face of the internment of Japanese Canadians during World War II; economic injustice and business ethics; and the challenges of the sexual revolution. On all of these issues, however, Berton notes the mainline church's lack of critical engagement, largely due to the cultural captivity described above. United Church critics also questioned the denomination's commitment to *diakonia* "when it fails to offer firm leadership, finds only $3 million a year for overseas work in a starving world, pens its clergymen behind tight white collars, confines local church activities almost entirely to self-serving social gatherings and fails to communicate properly its basic beliefs, even to its own members."[35]

For the United Church, the "new evangelism" was proposed as a response to the church's failings in the area of *diakonia*. Experimentation was to be encouraged, and engagement with the world outside the church was to be prioritized. In the essay, "Canadian Christians amid Revolution," penned by the editorial team from the Board of Evangelism and Social Service, a diverse array of possibilities are enumerated, including: forms of bi-vocational ministry, under the general description of "worker-priests"; community assistance programs and community service organizations; inner-city teen clubs and counselling services; pub theology; Christian ashrams and small group ministries; friendship houses; and work with those involved with prostitution or addictions.[36] The common factor in all of these suggested initiatives is the encouragement for the church to *go out*, to leave the safety of the stained glass harbor and risk engagement

---

34. Board of Evangelism and Social Service, *Why the Sea*, 39.
35. Board of Evangelism and Social Service, *Why the Sea*, 42.
36. Board of Evangelism and Social Service, *Why the Sea*, 48–54.

in the world. The church was being called to give itself away in service to the world. Giving itself away meant, in addition to stepping outside of its sanctuaries, removing the clerical collar and working to erase the markers that set the church apart from the world.

Doing so would offer the church "the golden opportunity to shed all connection with the power structure and return to the clean, uncluttered, uncompromising and selfless ideals of the early Christian martyrs, but in undated fashion."[37] These words are attributed to an unnamed respondent—identified as being under age 30 and having no religious affiliation—to a survey conducted of readers of *The Comfortable Pew*. They point to a theme that recurs repeatedly amongst the critics we are discussing; the suggestion is repeatedly made that there is a primitive core of Christianity that has been buried under unholy encrustations since the time of Constantine, and further, that agnostics might in fact be better, or truer, Christians than those who carry the name through formal participation in a congregation. The boundary between agnostics and those who were described as "religious" is one more boundary that is called into question. So Eric Nicol writes,

> The vertical schism between the orthodox believers and the non-orthodox humanists no longer serves the greater needs of humanity. It should be replaced by the horizontal division between men of good-will—call them Christianists, if the name serves—and those motivated by hate, fear, greed and the rest of the hellish demons that float freely through God's temples from Birmingham, Alabama to Cape Town.[38]

And from Berton:

> The thesis of this book is that the Christian philosophy and ethic has been shackled by its institutional chains; that "religion," as we know it today in all its organized manifestations, is something quite different from the Christianity of Galilee; that it tends to attract a different kind of person from the kind that followed the original precepts; that, in its desperate effort to preserve its established entity, the Church has become fossilized; and that this fossilization has prevented it from moving with the world.[39]

---

37. Hawkins, "Impact of a Record Best-seller," in Kilbourn, *Restless Church*, 160.
38. Board of Evangelism and Social Service, *Why the Sea*, 36–37.
39. Berton, *Comfortable Pew*, 115.

## CHAPTER 1. A STORY OF "THE SIXTIES"

The effort to retrieve the kernel of true Christianity from the religion in which it has become encased is also central to the secularists's critique of the *kerygma* of the church.

In discussing the church's failings in the area of *kerygma*, or proclamation, there is some irony in noting that it was precisely these kinds of "churchy" words that were the target of the secularist critics. The charge was made that "Words like 'immanent,' 'justification,' 'sanctification,' 'atonement,' 'witness,' 'substitutionary sacrifice' and many, many others are as obscure to non-churchgoers as the jargon of Madison Avenue is incomprehensible to the clergy."[40] Berton further asserts that maintaining a "special language of priesthood ... [is] an offence against the adulthood of the world."[41] Cox's theme of growing to maturity and casting aside tutelage emerges here. The sermon—characterized as "a speech which one man delivers and others passively accept"—also comes under critical review, with the suggestion that it be replaced by a dialogue, a drama, a debate, or a recorded presentation.[42] Here the critique is that the format is no longer appropriate to the modern communications age. The content of sermons is also found wanting:

> Where are the modern parables to fit the New Age? One rarely hears them from the pulpit, though one occasionally reads them in the newspapers, which seem sometimes to have usurped the function of the pulpit. The men in the pulpit seem content to retell the ancient stories, so many of which make no impact on a modern congregation.[43]

This critique of sermon content is set into the larger context of a discussion of dogma and doubt that is of central importance to secular theology. Berton commends Robinson's *Honest to God* for addressing issues of the credibility of biblical stories in the face of the findings of modern science. The church must be willing to subject its stories to scrutiny, and to acknowledge limits as to what it can know or claim about the mind or the will of God. There must be room for questions, for doubts; dogma may have to be abandoned altogether:

---

40. Berton, *Comfortable Pew*, 92.
41. Berton, *Comfortable Pew*, 93.
42. Berton, *Comfortable Pew*, 102.
43. Berton, *Comfortable Pew*, 99.

> What is wrong with the Church frankly admitting that there are many more specific things that it cannot know, but that there are some other things that it does believe: that it believes, for instance, truth is better than a lie, honesty better than a deceit, love and mercy better than hate and mistrust—that it believes in the general principles laid down by its founder and demonstrated by influential Christians across the ages.[44]

A critical shift is happening here—Christianity itself is being redefined. "General principles" are taking the place of specific content as the true core of the faith is retrieved from its dogmatic packaging. A kind of lowest common denominator religion is being promoted. So Berton argues, "To call a man an atheist because he does not believe in the virgin birth or the miracle of the loaves and fishes or the raising of Lazarus is to throw the baby out with the bathwater."[45] Later, in a concluding essay in *The Restless Church*, Berton adds: "I don't even think it is necessary to believe in such things to be a decent human being, to live a good, worthwhile and rewarding life, and even to be a 'Christian,' though that is a matter of semantics."[46]

The critique of the church's kerygmatic function moves from challenging obscure language, to challenging the authority of clergy and their monopoly on proclamation, and finally to challenging the content of the proclamation itself, with an agnostic claiming to have a better handle on the "general principles" of Christian truth than the church's authorized pastors and teachers. This last move does not appear to be grounded in secular theology as presented by Cox, who sets the discussion of *kerygma* within a relatively orthodox biblical framework. Noting that we live in a time between Easter Day and the Last Day, he writes:

> History is a permanent crisis in which the defeated old regime still claims power while the victorious new regime has still not appeared on the balcony. The New Testament looks forward not to the victory of Jesus, since that has already been won, but to the day when "every knee shall bow and every tongue confess" that Jesus is Victor.[47]

And yet, as we have seen, in this same discussion Cox relies heavily on the metaphors of growing up and taking responsibility: "man is invited to

44. Berton, *Comfortable Pew*, 113.
45. Berton, *Comfortable Pew*, 111.
46. Berton, "Dialogue with Myself," in Kilbourn, *Restless Church*, 191.
47. Cox, *Secular City*, 156.

make the whole universe over into a human place. He is challenged to push forward the disenchantment and desacralization which have expelled the demons from nature and politics."[48] This language seems to provide the license for critics like Berton and others to redefine the meaning of Christian faith.

## 1.3 A Critique of the Critics

> If you still don't believe in the Virgin Birth, etc., then I feel sure that you should have put in, say, twenty years farming.
>
> —A retired Manitoba famer in a letter to Pierre Berton[49]

It must be noted that, despite the popularity of books like *Honest to God* and *The Comfortable Pew*, opinions about Canadian mainline Protestantism in the 1960s were not monolithic. "Change was greeted in some quarters with enthusiastic approval, in others with hostility and even shock, and in still others with scepticism or an almost complete lack of interest," writes John Webster Grant, noting that support was strongest amongst the middle class, while blue-collar workers, farmers and people in business were far less enthusiastic.[50] Several of the contributors to *The Restless Church* pushed back hard against the arguments raised by Berton. William Stringfellow critiqued the thinness of Berton's theology: "The most cogent indictment of the churches which Berton's book makes is, in a sense, *himself* and his own Sunday School indoctrination in which he was misled, as so many others are, into supposing that the gospel is just a radical ethical idealism which should be applied to practical affairs in the world today."[51] Similarly, Eugene Fairweather writes from an Anglo-Catholic perspective:

> It is neither intelligent nor honest to use the word "Christian" as an honorific label for ideas or actions which a particular culture happens to like. The term stands for a response to a definite matter, derived from a particular history. Though there is room for advance in our understanding of God's word, as well as in our

---

48. Cox, *Secular City*, 155.
49. Berton, "Dialogue with Myself," in Kilbourn, *Restless Church*, 137.
50. Grant, *Church in the Canadian Era*, 200.
51. Stringfellow, "Case Against Pierre Berton," in Kilbourn, *Restless Church*, 24–25.

obedience to it, the Church's primary duty is to make sure that the content proposed to faith remains essentially the same.[52]

The battle lines are being drawn between an orthodox presentation of faith and a secularizing theology that tends towards agnosticism and humanism. In an essay titled, "The Relevance Bit Comes to Canada," Peter Berger upholds the enduring relevance and power of Christian tradition as a more effective response to social challenges than that offered by the new theologies of the secularists: "What would *really* be revolutionary would be to take seriously the beliefs of the New Testament, of the early Christian confessions, or of the sixteenth-century Reformers."[53] What Berger invites us to see is that the gospel is inherently relevant, and Christian tradition is rich with resources to respond to the challenges of each generation. These are the unique gifts the church has to offer the world: if the church were to set them aside or to drain them of their particular meaning in the pursuit of cultural relevance, what would be left of the church's witness as a church?

## 1.4 The United Church Responds

As we have seen, the United Church responded to the tumult of the 1960s with such initiatives as the New Curriculum and the new evangelism, and with the publication of the booklet, *Why the Sea Is Boiling Hot*. In the essays penned by the E&SS editorial team for the booklet, there is enthusiastic support for the changes demanded by the church's critics. The editorial team asks, "Isn't it time that the flame was turned up under this simmering church?," and later notes, "the challenge of involvement comes at the Church from all directions. It can no longer be denied. For the Church it is Hobson's choice, take up the challenge or end with nothing."[54] The team accepted the critique of the church's *kerygma* and acknowledged the need to address its "unintelligible jargon."[55] Even so, the editorial team's response stays within the bounds of Christian tradition and steers clear of the slip into agnosticism or humanism: "humanitarianism is not enough. . . . The hope of the Gospel does not finally rest in men but

---

52. Fairweather, "Catholic Tradition," in Kilbourn, *Restless Church*, 66.
53. Berger, "Relevance Bit Comes to Canada," in Kilbourn, *Restless Church*, 75.
54. Board of Evangelism and Social Service, *Why the Sea*, 38, 57.
55. Board of Evangelism and Social Service, *Why the Sea*, 41.

in the unbounded and inexhaustible love of God."[56] The critique of the church's *diakonia* would be addressed by the new evangelism that would drive the church out into service in the world. The new approach was an acknowledgement that "the Church has spent too much time verbalizing the Gospel and not enough time demonstrating it."[57] The new evangelism, formally expressed in the National Project of Evangelism and Social Action, would also address the United Church's shortcomings in the area of *koinonia*. Writing in the 1965 report of the Board of Evangelism and Social Service, Secretary Hord outlines three goals for the project: "to make the Church more relevant, by realizing that it is part of the world, charged with responsibility for the world"; to "push the Church out of her increasingly ghetto-like existence into living service in the world"; and, "to assist the Church to discover those forms of witness and fellowship which are required to make it effective in communicating the gospel in a rapidly changing social order."[58] These goals accord with the tenets of Cox's secular theology, with its call to responsibly engage the world, to contribute to its healing and reconciliation, and to allow itself to be transformed by the gospel which calls to it from God's future.

What was the longer term legacy of the United Church's response to its critics in the 1960s? Reflecting on the denomination's journey through this decade of ferment, Airhart suggests that "in many respects the church that was born in 1925 did not survive the tumultuous 1960s,"[59] and that its character was transformed by the impact of the mix of social, cultural, and theological forces that buffeted mainline Protestantism during the decade: "No longer could the United Church be counted as evangelical, in the contemporary meaning of the term—but neither could it truthfully be called Unitarian."[60]

I am persuaded by Airhart's assessment that the 1960s marked an ending and a beginning for the United Church of Canada, that the church born in 1925 did not survive the decade, and that a new United Church was brought to birth, one that survives to the current day. One symbol of the new church, born in the 1960s, is the United Church's New Creed, first adopted in 1968. In a poignant testimony to his "conversion," United Church minister

---

56. Board of Evangelism and Social Service, *Why the Sea*, 44.
57. Board of Evangelism and Social Service, *Why the Sea*, 41.
58. Board of Evangelism and Social Service, *Listen*, 106–7.
59. Airhart, *Church with the Soul of a Nation*, 256.
60. Airhart, *Church with the Soul of a Nation*, 290.

Edwin Searcy recalls studying the New Creed in his confirmation class the year it was adopted: "I notice that the church that has birthed me has, for the most part, continued along the path that it was on when I was confirmed. The place of the 'New Creed' in our church is an important sign that this is so. Since 1968 it has become, in practice, the only creed used in our denomination." Searcy characterizes this incarnation of the United Church as one marked by the desire to be "relevant" and "progressive," and suffering from symptoms of "amnesia." We have become unmoored from our story, and the eradication of "embarrassing words about the Father almighty, or the Virgin Mary, or the resurrection of the body, or the ascension into heaven" have left us with a thin theology ill-equipped to heal what ails us.[61]

## 1.5 Conclusion

> A generation from now will still another writer in another book be able to say that the Church in the Sixties continued to cater to the comfortable pew by ignoring the uncomfortable issues that lay just below the surface?
>
> —Pierre Berton, *The Comfortable Pew*[62]

This overview of the social, cultural, and theological milieux of the 1960s, and their impact on the United Church of Canada, is intended to focus attention on a number of matters that will be significant for the rest of this book. First, I have sought to demonstrate that the 1960s was a pivotal decade in the history of the United Church, the end of one conception of the denomination and the emergence of a new church birthed in response to the social, cultural, and theological ferment of the time. Second, more specifically, I have attempted to show that secular theology, as exemplified by Cox's *The Secular City*, had a significant influence on the shape of the United Church that emerged from the 1960s. The United Church of Canada heard the critique of secular theology, took its claims to heart, and responded in a robust manner, altering its educational programs, its approach to evangelism, and its theology.

From the vantage point of fifty years on, however, I note that many of the critiques of the mid-1960s could be repeated today without altering a single word (except for the substitution of inclusive language!). The

---

61. Searcy, "Story of My Conversion," 36–38.
62. Berton, *Comfortable Pew*, xxi.

same critique of the church's failings in the areas of *koinonia*, *diakonia*, and *kerygma* could be made. The United Church listened to its critics, and responded, but fifty years later the pews are as comfortable as ever. Many of our congregations still resemble those slightly boring luxury cruise ships, slowly drifting by a hurting world, oblivious to its cries. Too many of our congregations fail to reflect the diversity of the communities in which they are situated and remain enclaves of older, Caucasian, middle-class people, many of whom occupied the same pews fifty years ago.

One area that has seen dramatic change has been that of the form of presentation of the United Church's *kerygma*. The words that Berton lambasted as obscure in 1965 have largely disappeared from the lexicon of the United Church. Sermons generally are relevant, if not always scriptural. The format has changed, with many preachers eschewing the pulpit as a relic of a more authoritarian time and choosing instead to walk about amongst the congregation. Dialogue, drama, and the use of video presentation as alternate forms for sharing the message are not uncommon. Additionally, in the parts of the United Church with which I am familiar, the theology presented has moved in a more Unitarian direction, and dogma and doctrine as traditionally understood have become almost unmentionable words representing irredeemable concepts. And yet, I would argue, our radically altered presentation of the message has failed to rejuvenate our *diakonia* or reshape our *koinonia*. Our pursuit of relevance and the "progressive" label has not fundamentally changed the nature of our congregations from what they looked like fifty years ago. Even as we adopted the forms of the communication age and changed the content of our proclamation, we are preaching the gospel less and less frequently to fewer and fewer people.

The obvious question is, Why? How is it that all this change has left us in the same existential crisis the denomination faced fifty years ago? I believe that Airhart offers an important clue when she notes that the United Church's response to its critics in the 1960s did not result in a reversal to the church's pattern of numerical decline—and that doing so was not the intent of the proponents of change, the advocates of secular theology: "They were willing to risk theological anonymity and denominational invisibility when they took their faith into the wider community."[63] The willingness to risk anonymity and invisibility, to demonstrate the gospel rather than verbalize it, is a key move of secular theology. It represents the privileging of action over story, of behavior over belief, of service over formation.

63. Airhart, *Church with the Soul of a Nation*, 299.

Secular theology called people out of the sanctuaries, called clergy out of their collars and pulpits, and, lo and behold, the church ended up looking to all the world like a service club!

How did it go so wrong? It is my contention that the secular theology critics were correct in their assessment of the failings of the mainline Protestant church in the 1960s. I also affirm that Cox's typology of the essential marks of the church—*kerygma, diakonia,* and *koinonia*—remains a sound analytical tool for examining the proper functioning of the church. So, the tools were sound and the analysis looks correct. But what Cox, Berton, and the others could not have foreseen from their particular vantage point was the dramatic collapse of the cultural presence of Christendom. It is true that Cox and others detected the end of Christendom and the coming of the secular age, but the writers and thinkers of the time were still embedded in a cultural Christendom: even Berton, an agnostic who had ceased participation in the Anglican church decades earlier, could reel off the names of all the essential doctrines and dogmas!

When the advocates of secular theology called for anonymity and invisibility, coming out of the stained glass ghetto, and abandoning the particular language of the church, could they have imagined a world in which the church could actually disappear, and its story cease to be known? Those within the church were deeply committed to the Christian story; in seeking to demonstrate, rather than verbalize, the gospel, they could hardly have foreseen a world in which the basic Christian story might be unknown. They were challenging the hegemonic cultural power of the Christianity of their day; they were calling for the church to retreat from its role of Church, Inc.—official guardian of public morality and arbiter of civic virtue—and to assume a role more closely modelled on the humble and vulnerable church we meet in the pages of the New Testament. Helped by cultural forces, those who sought to challenge the power of the church succeeded beyond anything they could have imagined: the hegemonic Canadian mainline Protestant church of the 1960s was knocked off its pedestal and plunged into the boiling hot sea of a pluralist secular age.

In the 1960s the church's cultural and institutional power was seen as a barrier to its faithful practice of its core functions. In the increasingly secular age which has followed, a greater challenge for the church is the loss of its distinctiveness. Anonymity and invisibility, once seen as virtues, have become liabilities in a world of competing stories. We will turn now to an examination of the phenomenon of secularization.

## Chapter 2. Charles Taylor's Secularization Story

> Pierre Berton (echoing John Robinson) warned the churches of the 1960s that their decline was imminent due to their failure to keep pace with a changing society.... In short, the churches were on the losing side of history, fighting a doomed battle against progress and enlightenment.
>
> —KEVIN N. FLATT, *AFTER EVANGELICALISM*[1]

KEVIN N. FLATT OFFERS a summary of secular theology's critique and analysis of the mainline Protestant church of the 1960s as part of his discussion of the "secularization thesis." Flatt notes that the secularization thesis predicts the decline of religious practice as a consequence of processes of modernization and further notes that "despite the persistence of the secularization thesis, it has been convincingly challenged in recent decades on both empirical and theoretical grounds."[2] Given the persistence of the thesis in both the public imagination and academic environments, Flatt mounts an argument to show that the United Church of Canada's pattern of decline cannot be explained by the thesis. In his telling of the story, other factors are at play: the church's headlong embrace of secular theology, its acceptance of the "keep-up-or-die" warning, and its willingness to erase the boundaries between "church" and "world" were the key factors in the denomination's decline. Flatt cites the "subcultural identity theory of religious strength" advanced by sociologist Christian Smith, and its claim that vital churches in a pluralistic context exist as distinctive subcultures which both engage, and remain in tension with, the surrounding culture.[3] I will set to one side the question of Flatt's explanation of denominational decline,

---

1. Flatt, *After Evangelicalism*, 233.
2. Flatt, *After Evangelicalism*, 232.
3. Flatt, *After Evangelicalism*, 235.

however, and attend to the broader question of secularization theory. This chapter will present a summary of Charles Taylor's critique of the standard secularization thesis—as presented in *A Secular Age*—outlining its major themes with an eye to application to the story of the United Church of Canada. The chapter will conclude with some reflection on key themes in Taylor's work that have a particular bearing on our study.

## 2.1 The "Story" of Secularity 3

In the opening pages of *A Secular Age* Charles Taylor repeatedly describes the task he undertakes in the book as the telling of a story rather than the presentation of a straightforward argument based on analysis of the facts. "But why tell a story?" he asks, before answering, "Our past is sedimented in our present, and we are doomed to misidentify ourselves, as long as we can't do justice to where we come from. This is why the narrative is not an optional extra, why I believe that I have to tell a story here."[4] Taylor's main concern, then, is to tell a *corrective* story, a story that counters what he calls "subtraction stories":

> Concisely put, I mean by this stories of modernity in general, and secularity in particular, which explain them by human beings having lost, or sloughed off, or liberated themselves from certain earlier, confining horizons, or illusions, or limitations of knowledge. What emerges from this process—modernity or secularity—is to be understood in terms of underlying features of human nature which were there all along, but had been impeded by what is now set aside. Against this kind of story, I will steadily be arguing that Western modernity, including its secularity, is the fruit of new inventions, new constructed self-understandings and related practices, and can't be explained in terms of perennial features of human life.[5]

Taylor invites us to go beyond the standard narrative of subtraction stories, and to imagine a kind of "creation" story in which the conditions of modern belief are constructed over the span of five centuries, the period from 1500 CE to the present. Part of Taylor's agenda here is to honor this creation as an astounding human achievement, irrespective of whether one is inclined to embrace the secular age or mourn its advent.

---

4. Taylor, *Secular Age*, 28–29.
5. Taylor, *Secular Age*, 22.

## CHAPTER 2. CHARLES TAYLOR'S SECULARIZATION STORY

Taylor begins his story by setting out a taxonomy of secularity: what he terms secularity 1 concerns public spaces being "emptied of God, or of any reference to ultimate reality"; secularity 2 "consists in the falling off of religious belief and practice, in people turning away from God, and no longer going to Church"; secularity 3 describes "a move from a society where belief in God is unchallenged and indeed, unproblematic, to one in which it is understood to be one option among others, and frequently not the easiest to embrace."[6] The story Taylor will tell is his answer to the question posed by secularity 3: "How did we move from a condition where, in Christendom, people lived naively within a theistic construal, to one in which we all shunt between two stances, in which everyone's construal shows up as such; and in which moreover, unbelief has become for many the major default option?"[7] What makes ours "a secular age" is this notion of optional construals, our awareness that there are options for understanding the conditions in which we live; that these various construals are constructions we have created to make sense of our lives in the world; and that it is possible to live in one or another construal, or somewhere on the road in between them. We are not in Kansas anymore, and we are having profound doubts about the Wizard.

Within the wider story of how we came to live in secularity 3, Taylor is concerned with what he terms "fullness" or human flourishing: "we have moved from a world in which the place of fullness was understood as unproblematically outside of or 'beyond' human life, to a conflicted age in which this construal is challenged by others which place it (in a wide range of different ways) 'within' human life."[8] What is at issue here is discerning in a sense the "location" in which fullness may be found: is it to be located within us, within the bounds of ordinary human life, or is it something that calls to us from beyond? Taylor frames this question with the traditional terms of immanence and transcendence, and much of his story will center on the construction of what he names "the immanent frame" in which modern life is lived.

---

6. Taylor, *Secular Age*, 2–3.
7. Taylor, *Secular Age*, 14.
8. Taylor, *Secular Age*, 15.

## 2.2 The Process of Reform and the Construction of the Immanent Frame

For Taylor, the key driver of the creation of the modern secular age is the process of "Reform." As his account begins in the year 1500, this should not be surprising, but Taylor's term is to be understood to include more than just the Protestant Reformation and Catholic counter-Reformation narrowly defined. Describing the late medieval European world, Taylor notes that different members of society travelled at different spiritual "speeds": "What I'm calling 'Reform' here expressed a profound dissatisfaction with the hierarchical equilibrium between lay life and the renunciative vocations. . . . This equilibrium involved accepting that masses of people were not going to live up to the demands of perfection. They were being 'carried', in a sense, by the perfect."[9] Reform describes the drive to narrow the gap between the religiously perfect and the lay masses; Taylor understands this to be a kind of total program, operated on a society-wide basis, aimed at completely making over the spiritual lives of everyone. The various programs of Reform share a set of characteristics: they are activist, uniformizing, homogenizing, and rationalizing.[10] We cannot but be impressed at the sheer audacity of our forebears and their confidence in their powers to Reform human nature:

> This confidence is at the heart of the various programmes of discipline, both individual and social; religious, economic, and political, which begin to make us over from the sixteenth-seventeenth centuries. This confidence is consubstantial with the belief that we don't have to compromise, that we don't need complementarity, that the erecting of order doesn't need to acknowledge limits in any opposing principle of chaos.[11]

Chaos itself is banished in the new and highly disciplined order which emerges, and Taylor chronicles the efforts to "extirpate" the tradition of Carnival with its associations of excesses of the flesh and rituals of "misrule."[12]

The process of Reform has other consequences as well. It is necessarily a secularizing process, in that it is focused on human efforts to improve human behavior. The effort to narrow the gap between life in the monastery

---

9. Taylor, *Secular Age*, 61–62.
10. Taylor, *Secular Age*, 86.
11. Taylor, *Secular Age*, 125.
12. Taylor, *Secular Age*, 123–24.

## CHAPTER 2. CHARLES TAYLOR'S SECULARIZATION STORY

and life in the world involves the "sanctification of ordinary life" as a site of spiritual practice and the simultaneous downgrading of so-called higher forms of spirituality.[13] The net effect is to lower the bar in terms of what is expected from a faithful Christian: "this couldn't help but bring about a definition of the demands of Christian faith closer in line with what is attainable in this world."[14] Reform alters the dualistic conception of life in the world which had marked Christian understandings since the time of Augustine: "In the original medieval form, we have two spheres of life, with their proper activities and offices, corresponding to two 'cities' which coexist in history, the City of God, and the earthly city. . . . The process I have been calling Reform alters the terms of this coexistence; in the end it comes close to wiping out the duality altogether."[15] With its comprehensive scope, and its erasure of historic distinctions, the process of Reform takes us further in the direction of life lived within an immanent horizon with less and less reference to God who is growing ever more distant.

Ultimately, the relentless march of Reform results in the construction of "the immanent frame." Taylor describes it thus:

> So the buffered identity of the disciplined individual moves in a constructed social space, where instrumental rationality is a key value, and time is pervasively secular. All of this makes up what I want to call "the immanent frame". There remains to add just one background idea: that this frame constitutes a "natural" order, to be contrasted to a "supernatural" one, an "immanent" world, over against a possible "transcendent" one.[16]

Depending on perspective, one may read in(to) this description some of the limitations of the immanent frame that Taylor explores. It is disciplined and constructed, marked by instrumental rationality and pervasively secular time; it is this-worldly, having lopped off the supernatural and transcendent. It reflects a certain human cultural achievement; yet, as Taylor tells his story, the immanent frame starts to feel (for some) like a gilded cage. For some, life in the immanent frame provokes "a wide sense of malaise at the disenchanted world, a sense of it as flat, empty, a multiform search for something within, or beyond it, which could compensate for the meaning

---

13. Taylor, *Secular Age*, 179.
14. Taylor, *Secular Age*, 735.
15. Taylor, *Secular Age*, 265.
16. Taylor, *Secular Age*, 542.

lost with transcendence."[17] The problem for moderns is that we are at one and the same time aware of the limitations of older forms of belief—"the authoritarianism, the placing conformity before well-being, the sense of human guilt and evil, damnation and so on"—*and* unsettled by the limitations of the world we have constructed.[18] We are not much inclined to go back to the earlier dispensation, but the immanent frame leaves us asking with Peggy Lee, "Is that all there is?"[19]

The indictment of traditional religion and the modern quest for meaning in the face of an impersonal, mechanistic universe are themes we will explore further in subsequent chapters. What Taylor invites us to see is that denizens of the secular age are "cross-pressured," pulled in two directions, painfully aware that something is not right with our souls, but lacking clarity about where to go to heal what ails us. The world around us seems to offer a variety of competing options, jostling up against each other as they vie for our attention, and "fragilizing" one another in the process: "This mutual fragilization of all the different views in presence, the undermining sense that others think differently, is certainly one of the main features of the world of 2000, in contrast to that of 1500."[20] Another factor that continues to evolve, particularly as Taylor's story draws closer to our own time, is the association of humankind's "coming of age," or growing to maturity, with religious doubt:

> A religious outlook may easily be painted as one which offers greater comfort, which shields us from the truth of an indifferent universe, which is now felt as a strong possibility within the modern cosmic imaginary. Religion is afraid to face the fact that we are alone in the universe, and without cosmic support. As children, we do indeed, find this hard to face, but growing up is becoming ready to look reality in the face.[21]

This is also a theme to which we will return, as it is a central facet of the standard story of secularization. A particular subtheme of the "growing up" narrative from the time of Darwin to our own day focuses on the role of science in disproving religious belief.

---

17. Taylor, *Secular Age*, 302.
18. Taylor, *Secular Age*, 302.
19. Taylor, *Secular Age*, 311.
20. Taylor, *Secular Age*, 303–4.
21. Taylor, *Secular Age*, 364.

## CHAPTER 2. CHARLES TAYLOR'S SECULARIZATION STORY

Here Taylor draws attention to two kinds of believers who are particularly vulnerable: those whose "Christian faith was totally identified with certain dogmas or cosmic theories—e.g., the literal belief the Creation occurred in 4004 B.C.," and those whose faith may have remained at a "childish" level.[22] In the first case, science knocks the pins out from under a believing stance, and in the second, science makes its appeal based on its superiority to childish fables. In both cases, Taylor sees the convert retrospectively explaining the seemingly natural progression involved: "If I become convinced that the ancient faith reflects a more immature outlook on things, in comparison to modern science then I will indeed see myself as abandoning the first to cleave to the second."[23] The issue here is not with the inadequacy of faith per se, but with the limitations of an immature or overly literalist expression of it and its vulnerability to the lure of the idea of human progress. This calls to mind William Stringfellow's critique of the thinness of Pierre Berton's theology discussed in chapter 1.

Another aspect of the "growing up and taking responsibility" narrative of secularization is shown by the attraction of forms of Unitarianism in the eighteenth and nineteenth centuries. On this view,

> Jesus' role . . . is that of a teacher, by precept and example. His importance is as an inspiring trailblazer of what we will later call Enlightenment. For this he doesn't need to be divine; indeed, he had better not be, if we want to maintain the notion of a self-contained impersonal order which God in his wisdom has set up, both in nature and for human society.[24]

Here again we see a scaling back, a domestication of the divine, a retreat to within the human-centered immanent frame that will be important as our story develops.

## 2.3 From Mobilization to Authenticity

Taylor tells his story in more than one way. In addition to his thematic tracing of the impact of Reform and the construction of the immanent frame, he also presents a more tightly drawn historical narrative, designating historical periods as particular "ages." Taylor devotes considerable attention to

---

22. Taylor, *Secular Age*, 365.
23. Taylor, *Secular Age*, 365–66.
24. Taylor, *Secular Age*, 291.

two successive periods that he names respectively the Age of Mobilization (1800–1960) and the Age of Authenticity (1960–present). Taylor notes that the history of the past two centuries is the "terrain" on which the standard stories of secularization theory are told.[25] Here he is concerned with debunking the standard narrative that describes secularization as one long, steady, linear process of decline:

> an outlook which holds that religion must decline either (a) because it is false, and science shows this to be so; or (b) because it is increasingly irrelevant now that we can cure ringworm by drenches; or (c) because religion is based on authority, and modern societies give an increasingly important place to individual autonomy; or some combination of the above.[26]

Taylor concedes that certain parts of the secularization-as-an-inevitable-byproduct-of-modernization narrative are correct: "most of the changes they identify (e.g., urbanization, industrialization, migration, the fracturing of earlier communities) had a negative effect on the previously existing religious forms."[27] However, "it also happened that people responded to the breakdown by developing new religious forms," including Methodism,[28] and that "in a number of countries, religious practice rose in the nineteenth and sometimes also the twentieth century."[29] So the trajectory is not explained by a simple and straightforward equation of modernity and religious decline.

Taylor's journey through the last two centuries focuses on the hinge points at which each of the modern ages were born. The Age of Mobilization emerges around 1800 out of the *ancien régime matrix*, "an order of hierarchical complementarity, which is grounded in the Divine Will, or the Law which holds since time out of mind, or the nature of things."[30] It is this order which is undermined by the process of Reform. The Age of Mobilization "designates a process whereby people are persuaded, pushed,

---

25. Taylor, *Secular Age*, 423.
26. Taylor, *Secular Age*, 428–29. A drench is a medication used to treat ringworm in cattle, with the implication that technology has made appeals to divine intervention unnecessary.
27. Taylor, *Secular Age*, 436.
28. Taylor, *Secular Age*, 436.
29. Taylor, *Secular Age*, 424.
30. Taylor, *Secular Age*, 438.

dragooned, or bullied into new forms of society, church, association."[31] The new order that arises is named by Taylor as the "Modern Moral Order," which—unlike the *ancien régime* it displaces—does not consist in hierarchies or complementarities. Instead it is composed of "disembedded individuals" in "a society structured for mutual benefit, in which each respects the rights of others, and offers them mutual help of certain kinds."[32] At this point in Taylor's story the contours of our own world begin to emerge recognizably. This is the era and social matrix within which denominations (particularly in North America) and evangelical revivals are at home. Campaigns to combat drink, gambling, and promiscuity fit well within a reforming mindset that values the contributions of productive individuals to society. These efforts are part of the long history of Reform, which sought to raise the standards for everyone in society: "Evangelicals felt that they were fostering the ethos that their society needed to live up to its highest vocation and ideals. That's what gave them the confidence and sense of mission to demand that the whole society live up to certain of their standards, e.g., Temperance, and observance of the Sabbath."[33] It is this tightly constructed, rigorous moral order which comes unraveled at alarming speed in the 1960s, as "these tightly organized churches, often suspicious of outsiders, with their strongly puritanical codes, their inherent links, of whatever sort, to political identities, and their claims to ground civilizational order, were perfectly set up for a precipitate fall."[34]

This is the point in the story where Berton and the advocates of secular theology will feel right at home:

> If we think of the 60s as our hinge moment, we note a widespread critique of our society in the period immediately preceding it among leading intellectuals. The society of the 1950s was castigated as conformist, crushing individuality and creativity, as too concerned with production and concrete results, as repressing feeling and spontaneity, as exalting the mechanical over the organic.[35]

In contrast to earlier modes of conformity, the Age of Authenticity is marked by the emergence of "expressive individualism" as a mass phenomenon. Post-war affluence fuels a consumer revolution that coincides

---

31. Taylor, *Secular Age*, 445.
32. Taylor, *Secular Age*, 447.
33. Taylor, *Secular Age*, 470.
34. Taylor, *Secular Age*, 472.
35. Taylor, *Secular Age*, 476.

with a cultural mood that calls individuals to "do your own thing" in the context of a quest to "find yourself, realize yourself, release your true self, and so on."[36] Freedom of choice, along with concepts of "rights," "respect," and "non-discrimination," become the slogans of this age; but their meaning is trivialized and compromised by their entanglement with consumer culture and the focus on the self.[37] Spirituality in the Age of Authenticity is also cross-pressured, feeling the pull of both expressive individualism and consumer choice: "The religious life or practice that I become part of must not only be my choice, but it must speak to me, it must make sense in terms of my spiritual development as I understand this."[38] Finally, this is also the era of the sexual revolution marked by "the relativization of chastity and monogamy, [and] the affirmation of homosexuality as a legitimate option."[39] Each of these factors represent a challenge to, or rejection of, the values central to the Age of Mobilization, with its disciplined, society-wide campaigns of moral and social improvement. Together they work to comprehensively undermine that previous era and to unleash the particular secular age in which we now live.

## 2.4 Where We Live Now—The Age of Authenticity

One of the most important contributions that *A Secular Age* makes to the conversation about secularization and contemporary spirituality is Taylor's sympathetic reading of the spirituality of "the quest." The inspiration for contemporary seekers "often springs from a profound dissatisfaction with a life encased entirely in the immanent order. The sense is that this life is empty, flat, devoid of higher purpose."[40] Taylor notes the standard distinction which opposes "spirituality" and "religion": "This contrast reflects the rejection of 'institutional religion', that is, the authority claims made by churches which see it as their mandate to pre-empt the search, or to maintain it within certain definite limits, and above all to dictate a certain code of behaviour."[41] But rather than write seekers or questers off as superficial New Age dilettantes, Taylor places the spirituality of the quest

---

36. Taylor, *Secular Age*, 475.
37. Taylor, *Secular Age*, 477–79.
38. Taylor, *Secular Age*, 486.
39. Taylor, *Secular Age*, 485.
40. Taylor, *Secular Age*, 506.
41. Taylor, *Secular Age*, 508.

## CHAPTER 2. CHARLES TAYLOR'S SECULARIZATION STORY

within his larger historical narrative, as a contemporary form of reaction against the sterility of immanent frame. Questers are also in a sense heirs to the tradition of Reform: "The same long-term trend which produced the disciplined, conscious, committed individual believer, Calvinist, Jansenist, devout humanist, Methodist; which later gives us the "born-again" Christian, now has brought forth today's pilgrim seeker, attempting to discern and follow his/her own path."[42]

While noting that some forms of quest can indeed be exercises in self-absorption, Taylor cautions us against buying into dualistic polemics rooted in the "often raucous debate between those whose sense of religious authority is offended by this kind of quest, on one hand, and the proponents of the most self- and immanent-centred forms, on the other, each of which likes to target the other as their main rival."[43] These are the extreme points on a spectrum with authority at one end and unencumbered searching on the other, but Taylor wants us to notice that the debates that oppose "spirituality" and "religion" can lead us to completely misunderstand contemporary spirituality, and thus to miss opportunities to engage with those on the quest. Citing the examples of World Youth Day and the Taizé gatherings, Taylor suggests that the quest can often be an entry point to a life that may eventually incorporate more orthodox spiritual disciplines and religious practice. There is also a very practical side to Taylor's concerns here: whether or not we approve of contemporary forms of spirituality is to some degree irrelevant; this is the spirituality of our time and if we would reach people with the gospel, we need to do that within the framework in which we are living. We cannot simply click our heels and go back to an earlier time, nor can we wave a wand and change the ethos of the era in which we find ourselves. He also helpfully reminds us that the grass really is not any greener in any other historical dispensation: "If ours tends to multiply somewhat shallow and undemanding spiritual options, we shouldn't forget the spiritual costs of various kinds of forced conformity: hypocrisy, spiritual stultification, inner revolt against the Gospel, the confusion of faith and power, and even worse."[44]

A key characteristic of our current age is the retreat of Christendom, in which the "tight normative link between a certain religious identity, the belief in certain theological propositions, and a standard practice, no

---

42. Taylor, *Secular Age*, 532.
43. Taylor, *Secular Age*, 508–9.
44. Taylor, *Secular Age*, 513.

longer holds for great numbers of people."⁴⁵ Where Christendom has receded, patterns of "believing without belonging" or "diffusive Christianity" have become more common. Taylor notes that "churches have always had a penumbra around the core of orthodox, fully practising believers, whose beliefs shade off into heterodoxy, and/or whose practice was partial or fragmentary."⁴⁶ What has happened in the Age of Authenticity is that more and more people find themselves further and further out from the old core, "orbiting farther out from a star which is still a key reference point."⁴⁷ The links have been weakened, but there is still some kind of gravitational pull, which grows stronger on occasion (at times of national disaster, such as September 11, 2001) or in the presence of those who live lives of apparent sanctity.⁴⁸ Taylor wants us to see a "perspective of transformation"⁴⁹ at work here, the lingering lure of transcendence calling from beyond the immanent frame.

Taylor notes that "the retreat of Christendom involves both loss and gain."⁵⁰ As I mentioned at the close of the previous chapter, secular theologians of the 1960s had advocated for the retreat of Christendom in response to the Church's hegemonic social power, its too close association with the structures of what Taylor calls the Modern Moral Order. What Taylor invites us to see is that this retreat has opened up new possibilities for how Christians might engage in public discourse: "As the sense of living in Christendom fades, and we recognize that no spiritual family is in charge, or speaks for the whole, there will be a greater sense of freedom to speak our own minds, and in some cases these will inescapably be formulated in religious discourse."⁵¹ As Christianity relinquishes its hegemonic position, it can recover its original language and contribute its distinctive religious perspective in the public square. While there is risk inherent in the fact that each generation is orbiting further out from the star, even here Taylor sees hopeful signs: "The fading contact of many with the traditional languages of faith seems to presage a declining future. But the very intensity of the search for adequate forms of spiritual life that this loss occasions

---

45. Taylor, *Secular Age*, 514.
46. Taylor, *Secular Age*, 518.
47. Taylor, *Secular Age*, 520.
48. Taylor, *Secular Age*, 520–21.
49. Taylor, *Secular Age*, 521.
50. Taylor, *Secular Age*, 531.
51. Taylor, *Secular Age*, 532.

may be full of promise."[52] A distinctive church which maintains its peculiar language and some distance from "the world" may yet appeal to questers seeking relief from the sterile life within the immanent frame.

## 2.5 Excursus: The Gospel According to Charles Taylor

*A Secular Age* is not primarily a work of theology; the story Charles Taylor sets out to tell is instead a partial historical and philosophical account of the development of North Atlantic culture—and particularly the symbiotic relationship between Christianity and secularity—over the past five hundred years. In the closing chapters of the book, however, as Taylor attempts to work out the implications of his thesis, he offers some insights into his theological and ecclesiological perspective.

In a discussion of the variety of modern perspectives that seek to explain human nature, Taylor offers this summary of Christian belief:

> there are at least two key mysteries that Christian faith turns on: one is why we are in the grip of evil, why we were/are somehow incapable of helping ourselves to overcome this condition, and become the kind of creatures which we know we were made to be; the other is how the sacrifice of Christ broke through this helplessness, and opened a way out.[53]

Taylor urges intellectual modesty as to the extent of the claims we make about what can be known of these mysteries: "we have in a sense to operate with several different images in thinking of the mysteries of the Faith.... While each image adds something, it is only through a whole range of these that we can even distantly hope to capture something of God's work in the world."[54] For Taylor, God's initiative in Christ is the only thing powerful enough to get through to us, but our resistance to God remains, fueled by our awareness of the cost of a relationship with God: "our sin is our resistance to going along with God's initiative in making suffering reparative. We are deeply drawn towards God, but we also sense how following him will dislocate and transform beyond recognition the forms which have made life tolerable for us."[55] These descriptions of the mysteries at the heart

---

52. Taylor, *Secular Age*, 533.
53. Taylor, *Secular Age*, 651.
54. Taylor, *Secular Age*, 652.
55. Taylor, *Secular Age*, 655.

of Christian faith, and of the concept of sin, are important to Taylor's argument about the limits of the immanent frame and the necessity of an openness to transcendence.

The appeal to transcendence is part of Taylor's answer to the question he asks at the beginning of his story as to whether "fullness" might be found within the confines of an ordinary human life—within the immanent frame—or whether it requires participation in a relationship with the transcendent. At issue for Taylor is the search for adequate sources to motivate human transformation. The numerous processes of Reform attempt repeatedly to make over human nature, with limited success and a good deal of collateral damage. In the closing chapter of *A Secular Age*, Taylor engages Ivan Illich's exegesis of the parable of the Good Samaritan, finding within this story an alternative source for transformation. The saving action of the Samaritan

> creates a new kind of fittingness, belonging together, between Samaritan and wounded Jew. They are fitted together in a dissymmetric proportionality which comes from God, which is that of agape, and which became possible because God became flesh. The enfleshment of God extends outward, through such new links as the Samaritan makes with the Jew, into a network, which we call the Church.[56]

This is a picture of true *koinonia*, the church being the church in an embodied manner, putting itself on the line. The danger that such a church faces in the context of Reform and Mobilization is that it seeks to institutionalize, and thus depersonalize, its expression of *agape*: "in this way, we keep the hungry fed, the homeless housed, the naked clothed; but we are now living caricatures of the network life."[57] We will return to these themes in the discussion in chapter 5.

## 2.6 Summary—"A Secular Age" and Our Contemporary Dilemma

> Our faith is not the acme of Christianity, but nor is it a degenerate version; it should rather be open to a conversation that ranges over the whole of the last 20 centuries (and even in some ways before).
>
> —Charles Taylor, *A Secular Age*[58]

---

56. Taylor, *Secular Age*, 739.
57. Taylor, *Secular Age*, 739.
58. Taylor, *Secular Age*, 754.

## CHAPTER 2. CHARLES TAYLOR'S SECULARIZATION STORY

Having traced the outlines of the story Taylor tells in *A Secular Age*, we turn now to a review of a set of themes from Taylor's narrative that will be useful in our examination of the recent history of the United Church of Canada. I will focus on four themes: 1) Taylor's "correction" of the standard secularization thesis, including his refutation of its basic premise of inexorability and the narrative of subtraction; 2) the identification of secularity with a mature, responsible, "grown up" stance towards the world and the divine; 3) Taylor's positive assessment of the spirituality of the quest, and the opportunities for engagement it suggests; and 4) Taylor's suggestions for the role of orthodox expressions of faith in the context of pluralism.

As we saw in chapter 1, secularist critics of the 1960s mainline churches warned that "the Church must get with the world, or it will surely perish."[59] This statement encapsulates the basic premise of the secularization thesis, that secularization is an inevitable, inexorable part of the process of modernization. On this view, there is simply no place in a modern church for orthodox dogma or doctrine, or any place for the transcendent. Historical forms of Christian faith are simply incompatible with modernity. Taylor counters this view by showing that secularization is not a linear process, and that religious faith and modernity are by no means mutually exclusive. One quick glance at our contemporary geopolitical challenges ought to make this abundantly clear: religion remains a powerful source of motivation in our globalized world. Taylor offers a much more nuanced account here, showing that secularization and religious faith are more akin to fraternal twins, growing up together over the past half-millennium, influencing each other's development at every stage. Taylor's most powerful argument here is that "the immanent frame"—roughly equivalent to the secular world—is a construction, an astonishing achievement of North Atlantic Christian culture. As such, it represents an alternative "take" on reality, alongside the classical Christian understanding. It is, in a sense, an alternative religion; it most assuredly is *not* the truth about reality once all superstition has been expelled, as the standard subtraction thesis asserts.

Our second theme recalls secular theology's identification of secularization with growing up and taking responsibility for acting in the world. Here religious faith is strongly identified with a childish stance and immaturity. Secular humanity has come of age and is able—indeed *called*—to throw off the tutelage of religion and to step out into the glorious, sunlit clarity of the secular age. Taylor exposes the shortcomings that underlie

---

59. Berton, *Comfortable Pew*, 19.

this view, showing it to be the product of a combination of underdeveloped expressions of religious faith and a cultural bias that sees science is inherently superior to religion. Rejecting the view that science somehow disproves religion, Taylor instead asserts that when religion is shorn of the transcendent, and cut down to fit within an immanent framework, this very reduced, straw man expression of religion is vulnerable to the challenge of modern science.

On the positive side of the ledger, Taylor invites us to embrace the spirituality of the quest. Characteristic of the secular age and the retreat of Christendom are the emergence of a wide variety of spiritual and religious options and the rejection of earlier forms with their associations of conformity and authority. There is a connection here between what Berton termed the New Age and Taylor's Age of Authenticity. But where Berton and the secularist critics called for the church to "get with" the culture, advocating the renunciation of traditional moral teachings as well as the peculiar language and stories of the church, Taylor again offers a more nuanced view. He reads the quest as an unfulfilled hunger, a response to the sense of emptiness that arises in the immanent frame. The answer to this emptiness—what Taylor names fullness—is not to be found in the world that causes the hunger in the first place. For the church, offering more of what the world already offers (at better quality and for a lower price), trying to be more like the world, is not likely to meet the needs of questers.

There is also common ground between secularist critics of the church and Taylor, however. To the extent that the mainline church—the church of the comfortable pew—is embedded in its surrounding culture, it suffers from the malaise common to life in the immanent frame. Berton and the others are correct in naming the failings of such a church; Taylor offers a different prescription for addressing the issue. Rather than blend into the culture by erasing boundaries, Taylor suggests that a church offering a counterculture witness and modes of access to transcendence might be a more appropriate response to the spirituality of the quest. Taylor maintains an openness to the process of conversion, proposing that the church's role in the world might be best served by maintaining its traditions and practices, its peculiar language and story.

The fourth and final theme is related to this last point. Secularist critics in the 1960s advocated for a kind of "lowest common denominator religion" of "general principles" discerned from the life of Jesus recorded in the gospels and the lives of the saints throughout the ages. The particularities of doctrines and dogmas are seen as incompatible with modernity and an offence against the norms of democratic participation in a multicultural, pluralistic public sphere. This is a particularly important issue when one point of view is privileged, as the church was throughout history and into the 1960s, a privilege built up over centuries of sweeping programs of all-encompassing Reform. In such conditions, critics are right to call for limitations and constraints that allow other stories to flourish. But the conditions that have arisen since the retreat—in some areas, collapse—of Christendom have radically changed the church's relationship with non-Christians and with the culture as a whole. Taylor acknowledges the growing importance of religion as a source of motivation and inspiration in our secular age, and he sees the possibility of religious voices participating in a spirit of modesty and humility. Pluralism is often understood to require the silencing of religious language, but Taylor suggests ways that the church might engage non-hegemonically. Challenging the "all or nothing" posture of Reform, what Taylor calls for here is a respectful and wide-ranging conversation between and among the various construals to which he has drawn our attention.

These themes, and the questions they raise, will form the basis of our examination in subsequent chapters of proposed models for the United Church in our secular age.

## 2.7 Conclusion

> The churches were ripe for demythologization and the emptying out of the original generating power into what used to be called in Christian parlance, 'the world'. The world used up their virtues of duty, service and commitment to others, and then proceeded along its own calculating and utilitarian course, while every now and then regretting the loss of social capital, because it was so inconvenient.
>
> —David Martin, *On Secularization*[60]

Another prominent theorist of secularization, David Martin, offers this assessment of the impact of secularization on mainline Protestant churches in Canada in the twentieth century. To the extent that the churches reduced the boundaries between themselves and the surrounding culture, the churches

---

60. Martin, *On Secularization*, 98.

were swallowed up by that culture. This seems to confirm the analysis of Flatt with which this chapter opened. Yet there were compelling reasons for the United Church to make the decisions it did in the 1960s, and, after all, the numerical size of the church may not be the best measure of the church's fidelity to the gospel and to its Lord. In our next chapter, we will consider further the strategy of reducing the friction between the church and the world by examining a contemporary call for a "relevant" church.

## Chapter 3. Embracing the Culture's Stories

Give us this day our daily faith, but deliver us from beliefs.

—Aldous Huxley, *Island*[1]

The distinction between faith and belief, and the clear preference for faith over belief, is central to Harvey Cox's argument in *The Future of Faith*. This is a theme we will explore in this chapter as we critically examine the story of one particular United Church of Canada congregation, Calgary's Hillhurst United, and its minister, the Rev. Dr. John Pentland. It may seem unusual, perhaps even unfair, to select a single congregation and its key leader for such scrutiny. However, the reason for this selection is that Hillhurst and Pentland are frequently cited as outstanding examples of a congregation and a leader who are "bucking the trend" and achieving vitality and growth in an overall denominational context of diminution and decline. An arm of the United Church's national office published Pentland's recent book, *Fishing Tips: How Curiosity Transformed a Community of Faith*, and has hosted a webinar to bring the Hillhurst story to a church-wide audience.[2] Stories about Pentland and Hillhurst are also regularly featured in the *The United Church Observer*, the monthly denominational magazine, as well as in other media.[3]

Pentland has offered workshops based on *Fishing Tips* to United Church audiences across Canada as well as to a wider international audience. He

---

1. Quoted in Cox, *Future of Faith*, 213.
2. Pentland, *Fishing Tips*.
3. Some examples from *The Observer*: "Spirit Story" feature by John Pentland, March 2013; "The Hillhurst Effect: Inside a United Church Success Story," photo essay by Lyle Aspinall, November 2015; "Spiritual But Secular: Why Non-Believers Still Come to Church on Sunday," opinion piece by Anne Bokma, May 2016; "Spirit Story" feature by John Pentland, July 2016. Note that *The Observer* is an independently incorporated entity with its own editorial policies, and thus is not an official voice for the denomination.

appeared at the Skylight Festival (a Canadian version of the Greenbelt Festival) in the summer of 2016, and was scheduled to be the keynote speaker at an event co-hosted by the Vermont Conference of the United Church of Christ and the Center for Progressive Renewal in October 2016. Book study groups in a wide range of United Church congregations across Canada are meeting to discuss the ideas presented in the book.[4] Yet while the Hillhurst story has attracted much attention in United Church of Canada circles in recent years, Pentland makes clear that he is not offering a fully developed blueprint for ministry in a contemporary mainline context:

> It's my intention that this writing be a way of sharing our Hillhurst journey with others who might be interested in our change process and in what we've discovered. However, one of my worries in writing this book has been that it will be seen as a one-size-fits-all blueprint. It is not meant to be that, and can't be, a point I hope becomes increasingly clear as the book progresses. That is, the aim is never to achieve some spectacular result but always to inspire curiosity and a faithful creative process.[5]

It does not fall within the purposes of this study to assess the ministry of Hillhurst or the particular leadership strategies presented by Pentland in *Fishing Tips*. Instead, our examination will focus on the underlying principles and themes that Pentland brings to bear on his understanding of the challenges facing mainline congregations in our secular age. I will begin with a summary of Pentland's take on what it means to be a mainline congregation today, with reference to the work of two authors who serve as sources of inspiration to him: Cox and Diana Butler Bass. I will then critically examine Pentland's presentation using the four themes derived from Charles Taylor's work in *A Secular Age* and presented at the end of the last chapter.

---

4. A recent Internet search found workshops featuring Pentland in Victoria and Kamloops, BC; Lethbridge, Alberta; and London and Sarnia, Ontario; and book study groups in Victoria, BC; Ottawa and Thunder Bay, Ontario; Beaconsfield, Quebec; and Halifax, Nova Scotia. Pentland was also a keynote speaker in April 2016 at a conference cosponsored by the BC Conference and Kamloops-Okanagan Presbytery of the United Church and hosted by the congregation I serve, Trinity United Church in Vernon, BC.

5. Pentland, *Fishing Tips*, xiv.

CHAPTER 3. EMBRACING THE CULTURE'S STORIES

## 3.1 Fishing Tips: The Hillhurst Story

Pentland tells a story about the origins of Hillhurt's transformation from being a typical United Church of Canada congregation—fewer than a hundred in attendance, elderly, and in decline—to becoming the thriving and growing congregation it is today:

> One Sunday morning, pre-service, I was standing on the church front steps looking across the street at a restaurant that had people lined up out the door to get in for breakfast. I wondered, *What was that restaurant doing so well that people lined up to get in?* I wondered, *What would we need to do to have a line of people outside our doors?*[6]

Pentland continues the story by recounting how he shared this image and this question with the congregation in his sermon that morning, and was greeted by a chorus of gentle laughter. But he noticed something change in the room that day, as the congregation's prior work of planning and dreaming seemed to coalesce around this image: "Truth is, we'd been putting out ideas for some time; there was, however, something, maybe lots of things, resonant in *this* image that opened our hearts and imaginations. Some chord had been struck. I noticed; I felt it too."[7] This quest for a version of success, popularity, greatness, and relevance for the church is at the heart of the story Pentland tells. He recounts the statistics that document the United Church's numerical decline—attendance less than half of what it was twenty-five years earlier—and notes that "our influence has waned, and our spiritual lives are sidelined, and not only would we very much like back in the game, but the Prophetic voice calls us to try—to participate."[8] There is perhaps a hint of nostalgia here, for the days when the United Church of Canada had a robust and influential Social Gospel witness in Canadian society. Yet the quest for numerical strength also raises a series of questions: What does success for a church look like? Is the goal popularity, a full house on Sunday mornings? What other markers of success might we look to? In chapter 1, we noted Cox's criteria of *kerygma*, *diakonia*, and *koinonia* as the key functions of a church.

The fact that there is lineup on Sunday morning outside a restaurant, but not outside the church, leads Pentland to be curious about the

---

6. Pentland, *Fishing Tips*, 47.
7. Pentland, *Fishing Tips*, 47.
8. Pentland, *Fishing Tips*, 156.

distinctions or demarcations between church and culture. The restaurant is connecting with culture, offering something that appeals to customers, and that draws them out of their beds early on a Sunday morning. The church on the other hand is failing to connect to culture, failing to meet the needs of potential religious or spiritual customers, and is not seen to offer anything valuable enough to get out of bed for. This dichotomy suggests to Pentland that the church has lost its way, that it presents multiple barriers to participation to members of the public. Pentland wants to reduce these barriers, the "friction" that makes participation in church more difficult than participation in a restaurant meal: "we invite casual dress, contemporary songs, and we ensure that the line between church and culture is thin so that our faith isn't a Sunday thing, but a 24/7 experience—relevant anywhere."[9] One particular aspect of the distinction between church and culture that concerns Pentland is the notion of church as *separate* from, and *superior* to, culture:

> It's easy to separate church from culture. It's easy to see in our scriptures that culture is *distracting* at best, and so justify our separation. It's easy, all steeped in ideas, to imagine we take a road higher than that of culture, and so to see ourselves above it. Deep in our hearts we know this isn't true. I believe deep in our hearts we know that incarnation is the meeting of the secular and the divine. . . . I feel strongly that we need to honour the temporality of life and honour the people who live very meaningful lives in the so-called *secular* world.[10]

Pentland refers approvingly to the oft-quoted story in which Karl Barth advised preachers to "hold the Bible in one hand and the newspaper in the other" as a paradigmatic image of thinning the line between church and culture through relevance.[11] What Pentland—along with many others—neglects in his use of the image is the further qualification offered by Barth himself: "[Barth] recalls that 40 years ago he advised young theologians to 'take your Bible and take your newspaper, and read both. But interpret newspapers from your Bible.'"[12] Connecting with culture is an important

---

9. Pentland, *Fishing Tips*, 113.
10. Pentland, *Fishing Tips*, 154.
11. Pentland, *Fishing Tips*, 156.
12. "Quotes by Barth: What Did Karl Barth Say . . . ?," Princeton Theological Seminary Library, accessed April 18, 2016, http://www.ptsem.edu/Library/index.aspx?menu1_id=6907&menu2_id=6904&id=8450.

## CHAPTER 3. EMBRACING THE CULTURE'S STORIES

element of evangelism, but the newspaper and the Bible—the culture and the gospel—are not just two, interchangeable, equivalent stories according to Barth; the gospel interprets culture. Pentland appears to disagree, noting that "the history of the Church is just one stream in the history of human living, understanding and evolution, and, again for better *and* worse, it has played an irreplaceable role in the unfolding of culture."[13]

Pentland seems reluctant to draw any kind of line that would separate church from culture. In an article for the regular "Spiritual But Secular" feature in *The United Church Observer*, journalist Anne Bokma considers the question of what makes the church distinct from other kinds of community groups, especially for those who identify as "spiritual but not religious" (SBNR):

> Is church just a social club for these folks? So what if it is, says Rev. John Pentland of Hillhurst United, where many of the 450 congregants are SBNR and a full third are agnostic or atheist. Hillhurst has attracted the SBNR by "paying attention to the things they are talking about in coffee shops—their relationships and jobs and kids." Lots of churches, he says, talk about "stupid stuff." Instead, he preaches on decidedly non-religious topics ranging from the sexually graphic bestseller *Fifty Shades of Grey* to his "Reel Theology" series on popular films such as *Room* and *Spotlight*.[14]

In a recent workshop, Pentland reviewed a list of ten "shifts" that he observed occurring in the world of mainline Protestantism. Number six on the list was the shift from conceptualizing God as transcendent to conceptualizing God in immanent terms. He explained this shift in terms of the impossibility of believing in a transcendent God when one's prayers for divine intervention appear to go unanswered. Number ten on Pentland's list was the shift from "Spirit" to "soul," with the Spirit associated with transcendence, going beyond, and the soul with "descending, going inside, knowing myself."[15] The embrace of culture and the reluctance to admit a distinctive role for the church as a portal to transcendence suggest a grounded, this-worldly orientation for the church.

Further, Pentland's wholesale embrace of the secular is accompanied by an abiding unease with many aspects of the church and its traditions: "somewhere along the way we realized that we were actively undoing what

---

13. Pentland, *Fishing Tips*, 156.
14. Bokma, "In Church, Sort Of," 16.
15. John Pentland, Keynote Address.

it meant to be 'traditional' or 'churchy' church. Somewhere along the way we made the decision to be 'relevant.'"[16] Throughout the pages of *Fishing Tips*, and in presentations and interviews, Pentland draws on a repertoire of stereotypical, negative language for the church that echoes that of the secularist critics of the 1960s we encountered in chapter 1. Dogma and doctrine appear to have universally negative associations for Pentland. Thus, dogma is described as "exclusionary," something that gets in the way of taking care of one another, and something difficult to understand.[17] Dogma is "useless or irrelevant," and dogma and doctrine are antithetical to good worship practice.[18] Pentland is concerned that the language used in worship be readily understandable, that "rote recitation"[19] be dispatched, and that practices known only to insiders be kept to a minimum. Noting that "the word 'sermon' has gained a moralistic feel to it," Pentland opines, "given the chaotic and sometimes abysmal history of the Church, sermonizing on anything moralistic seems, right out of the gate, open to charges of hypocrisy for starters."[20]

The sacraments are made relevant and accessible, untethering them from centuries of ecumenical practice: "occasionally we have communion served in small baskets filled with grapes, rice crackers and chocolate in an agape feast style over conversation on the theme."[21] Pentland casts himself in the role of United Church iconoclast, challenging "liturgical legislation" and the denomination's bylaws as set out in *The Manual*.[22] He also invokes the conventional trope of the church's inquisitorial past: "for much of our Christian history, curiosity has not only been discouraged but persecuted. . . . On this point alone, you can see why science and religion might have parted ways."[23] As with the 1960s critics, there is a sense here that everything associated with church tradition is so tainted that it cannot be redeemed; it can only be radically transformed or discontinued altogether.

There is also a positive and constructive side to Pentland's work; it is encapsulated in his statement that "Hillhurst is intentionally aspiring to

---

16. Pentland, *Fishing Tips*, 57.
17. Pentland, *Fishing Tips*, 83, 86, 140.
18. Pentland, *Fishing Tips*, 178, 196.
19. Pentland, *Fishing Tips*, 205.
20. Pentland, *Fishing Tips*, 212.
21. Pentland, *Fishing Tips*, 208.
22. Pentland, *Fishing Tips*, 207, 225.
23. Pentland, *Fishing Tips*, xii.

## CHAPTER 3. EMBRACING THE CULTURE'S STORIES

be an Age of Spirit church."[24] The term "Age of Spirit" comes from Cox's *The Future of Faith*. It describes the post-Constantinian era of Christianity, whose birth pangs Cox discerns beginning around 1900 CE.[25] Pentland draws on Cox's distinction between belief as *opinion* and faith as *trust* to underscore the shift away from doctrine and dogma, and towards other organizing principles for the community of faith:

> Cox suggests that what people really want is to have access to the sacred without having to climb institutional or doctrinal scaffolding. They want a direct, intimate experience of God and Spirit, which doesn't mean they're at all happy about simply making it all up—it has to be real. That is, they're looking for both the way and the means of connection, of communion.[26]

Pentland also draws inspiration from Diana Butler Bass's presentation of "three dimensions of religion"—believing, behaving, and belonging—in her work, *Christianity After Religion*.[27] Of particular interest here is Bass's understanding of how these dimensions are interrelated:

> She says it used to be that people *believed things about God*, and that was good: they had done their work. They had learned the rules—what to wear, when to stand or sit, what parts to say and what parts to remain silent through. All this understood, then they belonged. *Believe—Behave—Belong*. She suggests the pattern now is reversed: *Belong—Behave—Believe*. Belonging as the *starting* place of the spiritual journey. *Are we creating safe places where this Age of Spirit can unfold?*[28]

For Pentland, "our task is to provide a safe and hospitable environment for the *seeker* to stay a while, to explore."[29] We are in the territory of the *spirituality of the quest* identified by Taylor. At the heart of Pentland's Age of Spirit church is hospitality towards the quest for meaning and purpose: "we want to discuss what people everywhere discuss—*life*: where we fit, what it means, how we can help ourselves and others in a way that is fruitful, how

---

24. Pentland, *Fishing Tips*, 56.
25. Cox, *Future of Faith*, 7.
26. Pentland, *Fishing Tips*, 55.
27. Bass, *Christianity After Religion*, 47. Note: this work is incorrectly cited as *Christianity For the Rest of Us*, another Bass title, in *Fishing Tips*.
28. Pentland, *Fishing Tips*, 56.
29. Pentland, *Fishing Tips*, 72.

we can engage what is larger than our own selves, what is our purpose."[30] *Meaning* is a central theme for Pentland, one that he connects back to the life of Jesus: "Jesus was fundamentally about how to have a meaningful life."[31] He also acknowledges that Jesus can be a problem for the Age of Spirit church:

> We have wrestled long and hard in modern times with what to do with Jesus—how to understand him, how to "read" what he said and did, how to have faith in and with him. On one extreme, some of us cling unflinchingly to an understanding that, literally, poses a lot of cognitive trouble for a lot of people. On the other, some people have called for a moratorium on any talk of Jesus at all, which, to my sensibility, opens up a sad, uncomfortable, even untruthful void. In any event, both sides (and other sides as well) throw the baby out with the bathwater, leave us lacking something.[32]

As always with the baby and the bathwater analogy one must ask, Which is the baby and which the bathwater? What is central and what is ancillary? Is the person of Jesus ancillary to the central issue of meaning, with Jesus as an exemplar or paradigm of a meaningful life; or is Jesus the proverbial baby, the irreplaceable, unreducible heart of our faith?

In summary, this review of the Hillhurst story has focused on four elements: Pentland's vision of a popular and relevant church with a lineup outside its doors; the thinning, or erasure, of the line that separates church from culture; a negative and stereotypical view of church tradition, dogma and doctrine, and historical practices; and the aspiration to be an "Age of Spirit" church organized around the quest for meaning. Our next task is to examine these elements in light of the four themes derived from Taylor's work in *A Secular Age*. However, before turning to that task, it will be helpful to consider more closely some of the ideas and themes presented by Cox in *The Future of Faith* and Bass in *Christianity After Religion*, as these provide some of the key theological underpinnings for Pentland's work.

## 3.2 Excursus: "The Age of the Spirit"

The Age of Spirit is the third Age in Cox's typology, following the Age of Faith (from the time of Jesus to the time of Constantine) and the Age of

---

30. Pentland, *Fishing Tips*, 155.
31. Pentland, Keynote Address.
32. Pentland, *Fishing Tips*, 102.

CHAPTER 3. EMBRACING THE CULTURE'S STORIES

Belief (the centuries from the time of Constantine up to the modern era). Cox understands the "faith" of the first age to be centered in the community's "hope and assurance in the dawning of a new era of freedom, healing, and compassion that Jesus had demonstrated."[33] The subsequent Age of Belief arises as church leaders develop primitive instructional programs to guide the formation of subsequent generations of Christians: "emphasis on belief began to grow when these primitive instruction kits thickened into catechisms, replacing faith *in* Jesus with tenets *about* him," a process intensified and further hardened during the ecumenical councils.[34] We see here a theme identified in chapter 1: the notion of an original, "pure" form of Christianity that subsequently becomes encased in the trappings of the church—dogmas, doctrines, and ecclesiastical hierarchies—and that must be retrieved. While noting that we cannot go back to an earlier time or recreate a lost world, Cox advocates an ecclesiastical version of the contemporary concern with domestic decluttering: "Can we preserve the jewels and get rid of the junk?"[35] It should be noted that Cox's narrative of the Age of Faith rests upon the somewhat dubious claim that "chronologically the *Gospel of Thomas* is as 'original' as Mark's gospel and may be even more 'original' than the Gospel of John,"[36] and upon the scholarship of Karen King, the leading proponent of the now-discredited *Gospel of Jesus' Wife*.[37]

For Cox, much of the blame for what went wrong during the Age of Belief is ascribed to the development of creeds. He draws a continuous line from small adjustments that began to be made in the decades after Jesus' life and ministry, to the "permanent pattern" of creed-making that emerged in the third and fourth centuries, through to the Reformation's competing Confessions, and to Fundamentalism in the modern period.[38] Creeds tend to function as boundary markers, fences that determine who is included in the family of faith and who is excluded, rather than as aids to deepening faith. The language of creeds is literalized, hardened into propositions to which one must assent. They become dogma and doctrine, experienced

---

33. Cox, *Future of Faith*, 5.
34. Cox, *Future of Faith*, 5.
35. Cox, *Future of Faith*, 184.
36. Cox, *Future of Faith*, 87.
37. Cox, *Future of Faith*, 65, 225. For background information on the *Gospel of Jesus' Wife* see http://gospelofjesuswife.hds.harvard.edu/introduction. Accessed August 3, 2016.
38. Cox, *Future of Faith*, 74.

as systems of codes and rules and restrictions, devoid of meaning and drained of the transforming power of story or poetry. Against this backdrop, spirituality is powerfully and persuasively attractive. Cox cites three reasons for its popularity:

> First, it is still a form of tacit protest. It reflects a widespread discontent with the preshrinking of "religion," Christianity in particular, into a package of theological propositions by the religious corporations that box and distribute such packages. Second, it represents an attempt to voice the awe and wonder before the intricacy of nature that many feel is essential to human life without stuffing them into ready-to-wear ecclesiastical patterns. Third, it recognizes the increasingly porous borders between the different traditions and, like the early Christian movement, it looks more to the future than to the past.[39]

Cox presents spirituality as largely a "protest" against the limitations of Taylor's immanent frame and the rigors and restrictions of the programs of Reform. At the same time, Cox's Christology—like Pentland's—appears to be confined to the immanent frame and limited to a particular understanding of the meaning of Jesus' life and teachings: "the stories of the Resurrection, as hard as they are for modern ears to comprehend, mean that the life Jesus lived and the project he pursued (the Kingdom of God) did not perish at the crucifixion, but continued in the lives of those who carried on what he had begun."[40] That is *a* meaning of the Resurrection, but it is one that rests comfortably inside the immanent frame, truncating possible transcendent meanings.

In *Christianity After Religion*, Diana Butler Bass also focuses on the spirituality/religion dichotomy, presenting a word association chart derived from her workshops with clergy, church leaders, and church members across North America and in Australia. As might be expected, the "religion" list features *institution, rules, authority, boundaries,* and *hierarchy;* as well as the well-worn *dogma* and *beliefs*. The "spirituality" side of the ledger contains the words *searching, experience, connection, open,* and *inclusive;* along with *prayer, nature,* and *transcendence*.[41] Here again we can detect the association of religion with the immanent frame and the processes of Reform, while spirituality is cast as a form of resistance and an aspiration to

39. Cox, *Future of Faith*, 13–14.
40. Cox, *Future of Faith*, 52.
41. Bass, *Christianity After Religion*, 69.

break out of the restrictions. This should perhaps not surprise us, given that the form of religion most familiar to us is that of Taylor's Age of Mobilization (1800–1960) with its society-wide campaigns of moral reform and its emphasis on civilizational order.

What Bass calls for is a rehabilitation of the concept of religion, recovering its etymological origins in *religio*—to reconnect—and its premodern definition, which suggested something closer to the concepts of faith, trust, and love.[42] Like Cox and others, Bass makes an appeal for a retrieval of aspects of the "original" Christian faith and sets her triad of *believing—behaving—belonging* within the framework of a return: "Christianity of the Great Returning is the oldest-time religion—reclaiming a faith where belief is not quite the same thing as an answer, where behavior is not following a list of dos and don'ts, and where belonging to Christian community is less like joining an exclusive club and more of a relationship with God and others."[43] Here there is perhaps an echo of Cox's marks of the church described in chapter 1: *kerygma* (belief), *diakonia* (behavior), and *koinonia* (belonging). What comes across more strongly in Bass's book than in Pentland's use of it is this commitment to rehabilitating religion, including redeeming practices and forms, rather than choosing to relegate whole aspects of religion to the ash heap of history.

## 3.3 "Charles Taylor, Meet John Pentland"

At the end of chapter 2, we considered four themes drawn from the story told by Charles Taylor in *A Secular Age*. These four themes will supply a template to guide our evaluation of John Pentland's presentation of the Hillhurst story. The four themes are: 1) Taylor's "correction" of the standard secularization thesis, including his refutation of its basic premise of inexorability and the narrative of subtraction; 2) the identification of secularity with a mature, responsible, "grown up" stance towards the world and the divine; 3) Taylor's positive assessment of the spirituality of the quest, and the opportunities for engagement it suggests; and 4) Taylor's suggestions for the role of orthodox expressions of faith in the context of pluralism.

Our first theme from Taylor is foundational; it sets the parameters for the discussion of secularization and modernity and their impact on faith communities. Taylor's focus is on what he names secularity 3, the situation

---

42. Bass, *Christianity After Religion*, 97.
43. Bass, *Christianity After Religion*, 99.

in which belief in God "is understood to be one option among others, and frequently not the easiest to embrace."[44] He is concerned with the background "conditions of belief," the social, cultural, and philosophical matrix within which faith communities vie for attention, resources, and commitment. Taylor sees this matrix—which he names the immanent frame—as a construction, a human creation, in contrast to the standard "subtraction stories" of secularization theory, which portray modernity as the move out of a benighted past and into the light of clear-eyed reason. Taylor cautions us against accepting uncritically a linear narrative of progress, in which each age is superior to what went before it, and instead suggests something more akin to the parable of the wheat and the weeds, in which our forms of religious belief and the conditions of modernity are intertwined and in some sense inseparable. Additionally, the implications of all of this are that modernity and the immanent frame can be experienced both as liberating and constricting; they give and they take away. In our secular age, modernity and religion mutually fragilize one another, undermining each other's hegemonic claims, casting doubt on the all-sufficiency of either option. What this also strongly suggests is that the prospects for recovery of a pure, or original, religious stance unsullied by all-too-human aspirations and foibles are extremely doubtful.

From the sources available to us, it is not possible to reconstruct a full and complete picture of the philosophical and theological underpinnings of Pentland's approach to ecclesiology. As noted at the beginning of this chapter, Pentland is clear that he is not offering a comprehensive blueprint or model for ministry. But what can we glean from the information available to us? To begin with, Pentland's vision of a popular church seems to be a response to what Taylor names as secularity 2, "the falling off of religious belief and practice, in people turning away from God, and no longer going to Church."[45] Hillhurst is regularly cited in the media as a model United Church congregation that is bucking the trend, and a consistent part of telling the Hillhurst story is sharing its "numbers"; Pentland points to evidence of growth in worship attendance, Sunday School participation, financial contributions, staff size, and demographic diversity as indicators of the transformation the community has undergone.[46] Hillhurst's numerical growth and demographic diversity are taken as signs

44. Taylor, *Secular Age*, 3.
45. Taylor, *Secular Age*, 2.
46. Pentland, *Fishing Tips*, xv.

of its success, and in the context of general denominational decline and aging, Hillhurst stands as an oasis in the desert for thirsty and weary congregations. The Hillhurst numbers play no small part in the ongoing attraction to, and fascination with, the congregation and Pentland in the United Church of Canada and beyond, as evidenced by the publication of *Fishing Tips*, frequent *Observer* articles, numerous book studies, and Pentland's long list of speaking engagements.

Though Pentland may not intend it, the showcasing of numbers can easily fuse with a lingering nostalgia for an earlier era in the United Church's history. We saw previously how Pentland expresses a desire to get "back in the game" and recover some of the United Church's lost social, cultural, and political influence. Admittedly, Pentland also sees this as a prophetic call—it is not just growth for growth's sake—but the call for a culturally influential church sounds suspiciously close to a return to some earlier form of Christendom. Pentland clearly has good intentions, but as his reflections on church history suggest, good intentions can go astray, especially when they are not tempered by the qualities of Christian humility rooted in the story of the life, death, and resurrection of Jesus Christ.

Pentland's call for the thinning, or erasure, of the boundary line between church and culture, his wholesale embrace of the secular, seems to come close to Taylor's conception of secularity 3 in which religion and modernity are intertwined and inseparable. But where Taylor posits that religion and secularity exist in tension with each other, mutually fragilizing but also enriching each other, Pentland wants to marry the two together, seeing religion as one amongst many cultural streams. This is part of Pentland's shift to the immanent and the inner as the only appropriate terrain for religion. This recalls Taylor's chronicle of the processes of Reform that aim to narrow the gap between the spiritual realm and the secular. Taylor cites Augustine's "two cities"—the City of God and the earthly city—and notes how Reform continually attempts to narrow and almost eradicate the gap:

> If one carries this rapprochement of the two orders to its ultimate end point, one falls into a kind of Deism, in which the Incarnation loses its significance, Jesus becomes a great teacher expounding the demands of God, and what these demands consist in is a morality which allows us to live here in peace and harmony, a version in other words of the modern moral order.[47]

47. Taylor, *Secular Age*, 735–36.

For Taylor, Reform's narrowing of the gap comes with a sense of lowering the bar in terms of what is expected from a faithful Christian life, to allow for wider participation. In a webinar presentation of the material from *Fishing Tips*, Pentland was asked a question about the church's countercultural witness. He responded, "It's not like we have a sacred and a secular world; we have one world and it's sacred." Speaking of the church's prophetic critique of government and business, Pentland affirmed the positive qualities of those institutions, adding, "I'm just a fan of saying, 'We're all in this together,' and let's not alienate people."[48] There is one world, and it is sacred, but it is also enclosed within the immanent frame, within which we are called to live in peace and harmony without alienating one another. Ultimately, Pentland does not seem to have a need for, a use for, or a place for the transcendent in his ecclesiology. He responds to the constraints of the immanent frame by going within and engaging the quest for meaning as we will see below.

Our second Taylorian theme is the identification of secularization with growing up and taking responsibility for acting in the world. Here Taylor dissects the hackneyed trope that says modern science has disproved religion, freeing us from childish superstition. Taylor identifies childish faith and literalism as factors contributing to a weakened faith stance which is unable to withstand the volleys aimed at it by scientific truth. In the post-Enlightenment period, two developments come together: on the one hand, a straw man caricature of religious faith starts to take hold; and on the other, an awareness of human power and potential begins to dawn. Humanism arises out of Christian faith, but as it grows to maturity, it comes to look upon its parent with sneering disdain.

This disdain is apparent in Pentland's work as he repeats, seemingly uncritically, the most common negative stereotypes of the church and religion advanced by humanist critics across the centuries. The humanist caricature of the church appears to have a powerful hold on Pentland's imagination, leading him to take on the role of unrelenting critic of dogma and doctrine in a church in which dogma and doctrine seem to have very little life or force, outside of the imagination of critics like Pentland. At one point in *Fishing Tips* Pentland offers this description of Hillhurst: "So there we are, inside looking out. A group of people pretty determined not to escape this world for some idealized better one."[49] The implication seems to

---

48. Pentland, *Fishing Tips* (webinar).
49. Pentland, *Fishing Tips*, 159.

## CHAPTER 3. EMBRACING THE CULTURE'S STORIES

be that there are other Christians who hold to an other-worldly spirituality and that Hillhurst's this-worldly orientation is the better path. Otherworldly spirituality is not a commonly travelled path in the United Church with its strong Social Gospel and theologically liberal heritage. It is possible that Pentland is referring to non-United Church Christians here, particularly those who are labelled "Evangelical" or "Fundamentalist" Christians in common United Church usage. In any case, we are dealing with an unhelpful, unfair, and uncharitable stereotype or caricature here.[50]

There are no doubt helpful and useful criticisms that can be made about church practices and traditions. An incarnational church is necessarily enmeshed in a mixture of human foibles and aspirations. But Taylor reminds us to do our homework and engage in critiques that are rooted in a more nuanced appreciation of the messiness of incarnation. We do ourselves and the church no service by repeating hackneyed stereotypes. We can instead identify problems, detect their sources, and work at necessary course corrections. Here our review of Bass's delineation of spirituality and religion is helpful, reminding us as it does of the impact of the Age of Mobilization on our religious forms. When we do the work of teasing apart what is a cultural pattern from what is the essential core of our faith, we discern what indeed is baby and what is bathwater and can make better choices about the future. While it is true that there is no returning to a pure, unadulterated faith for Taylor—since religion and culture are always intertwined—we are called to an ongoing discernment through history of the ways in which our faith is incarnated in particular cultural contexts. Without careful discernment there is a danger that an anti-dogma stance becomes a new dogmatism.

Our third theme is the spirituality of the quest and here is where there is potential for the greatest affinity between Taylor and Pentland. Taylor cautions against a traditionalist or orthodox dismissal of the spiritual quest as self-absorbed and invites communities of faith to adopt a stance of hospitality towards seekers. Pentland's aspiration that Hillhurst be an "Age of Spirit" church accords well with Taylor's positive regard for the spirituality of seekers. Taylor understands the spirituality of the quest as both a reaction to the sterility of the immanent frame and an heir of the processes of Reform, as questers seek forms of spiritual enrichment and new disciplines and practices. A key issue for Taylor in regards to the quest is his openness

---

50. During my time studying at Duke Divinity School, I regularly encountered United Church stereotypes that express disdain for "Southern" or "American" Christians.

to the possibility of conversion. We all live within the immanent frame—the issue is whether or not our worldview is "open" or "closed" to the possibilities of transcendence.

Drawing on the work of Cox and Bass, Pentland picks up on the malaise that inspires the spiritual quest and he is keen to reduce or remove barriers that get in the way of questers's participation in the life of the community of faith. He describes the theological makeup of the Hillhurst congregation as comprising one-third of participants with a United Church background; one-third from Catholic, evangelical, or other Christian backgrounds; and one-third agnostic or atheist. Pentland recommends this as an appropriate theological profile for congregations since our cultural context is "anti-religious but open to the Spirit."[51] Pentland employs Bass's reversed *Belong—Behave—Believe* triad to invite seekers and questers and questioners into community participation. The focus for Pentland is on creating "safe spaces" for exploring meaning. As noted above, however, Pentland understands the quest to take place within the immanent frame: the quest for meaning takes a horizontal form, in conversations between individuals, or involves a journey within, an encounter with one's soul.

Taylor recognizes the search for meaning as a consequence of the narrowed horizons of the immanent frame, but he sees it as a kind of modern, first-world problem: "You couldn't even have explained this problem to people in Luther's age. What worried them was, if anything, an excess of 'meaning', the sense of one over-bearing issue—am I saved or damned?—which wouldn't leave them alone."[52] The concern over meaning arises within the context of modernity and disenchantment, the advent of individualism, and the perceived loss of access to the transcendent. For that very reason, the *solution* to the question of meaning cannot be found within the immanent frame. For Taylor, the spirituality of the quest involves opening a portal to the transcendent. Communities of faith ought to be attentive to, and open to, the needs of seekers. But they also need to be inviting seekers into the possibility of conversion, a spiritual journey that in its most important aspects is between the individual and God. In this process, however, the community is holder of the story, the keeper of the map that shows the way-markers others have trod. The community is the communion of saints engaged with God in the process of making more saints.

---

51. Pentland, Keynote Address.
52. Taylor, *Secular Age*, 303.

## CHAPTER 3. EMBRACING THE CULTURE'S STORIES

Taylor notes, "part of what it has normally meant for the patterns and cycles in my life to have meaning and validity for me is that they are those of my forebears."[53] The gospel and Christian tradition offer patterns of obedience within which questions of ultimate meaning are either answered or given a framework, orientation, or pattern. Questers in the Age of Authenticity—the era of expressive individualism—are inclined to reject traditional patterns as too constraining of their freedom. Having rejected the set of meanings provided by the gospel and Christian tradition, they engage in a quest for meaning in a world of competing narratives. This can all too easily deteriorate into a form of consumerist spirituality in which questers themselves determine the extent to which they will engage: submission or obedience to patterns set by others are out of the question; the individual's freedom to choose must remain sovereign. The potential problem with the form of community proposed by Pentland is that quests for meaning may remain shallow and self-centered, truncated by a resistance to the gospel engendered by a reluctance to commit to a path. Without a story that offers the possibility of a portal to transcendence and a new way of life, such a community may keep people trapped in endless wilderness wandering in search of meaning. The lesson here is that when a Christian community no longer speaks its particular language, or tells its particular story, or recites its historic creeds, or engages in practices that are recognizably part of a wider tradition, it is hard to see how it can offer helpful resources to those pushing up against the limits of the immanent frame. In the Age of Authenticity the challenge for communities is to maintain both an openness to the spirituality of the quest *and* a pathway that is open to the possibility of transcendence. This requires a willingness not to foreclose options on the one hand, and, on the other, to stay connected and rooted in a particular story and tradition.[54]

Our fourth and final theme from Taylor addresses the challenge of pluralism: how is it possible to tell a distinct and particular story in a world of competing narratives and contested meanings, and to do so in a manner that is respectful towards other points of view? The end of Christendom and the combined impacts of secularity 1, 2, and 3 on the North Atlantic world have vastly curtailed Christianity's cultural power. Yet, contrary to the predictions of some proponents of secularization in the 1960s, religion has not disappeared as a powerful, motivating cultural force. The Christian

---

53. Taylor, *Secular Age*, 719.
54. Taylor, *Secular Age*, 512.

perspective is now one perspective among many in the public arena and in the spiritual marketplace. According to Taylor, our times call for a respectful dialogue between faith and belief positions: "I think what we badly need is a conversation between a host of different positions, religious, nonreligious, antireligious, humanistic, antihumanistic, and so on, in which we eschew mutual caricature and try to understand what 'fullness' means for the other."[55] The end of Christendom provides an opportunity for humble and respectful conversation, but in order for that to happen the church needs to have clarity about what it believes and what is essential to its story. This requires a teasing apart of the essence of Christian faith from its cultural packaging. It requires the cultural disestablishment of religion. In many respects our secular age has created the ideal conditions for this to happen, but we need to take up the opportunity that is offered to us. We need to be willing to engage in the work of retrieval and we need to be willing to be a countercultural church, a church that understands the ways in which it must be distinct from its host culture. This is a particular challenge for the United Church of Canada, which has been so deeply embedded in Canadian culture and enmeshed in the history of Canadian nation building. It is part of the denomination's DNA to see itself as the benign face of mainline Canadian Protestantism.

Pentland's stance towards culture does not permit a countercultural orientation for the church. He recounts the story of his ordination in a university gymnasium:

> There, above me, on the gymnasium wall, was a banner. It read, "*Adidas, we are with you all the way!*" I smiled. Now, 28 years later, I wonder whether this was a marriage of culture and church that 'lay its hands upon me' too, for this precise theme has carried through all my ministry and career: *Adidas*, the running shoe symbolically moving me into culture, while I was carried Spirit-wise by the words "*we are with you*" which I heard alongside the great commissioning in Matthew's gospel, "Lo, I will be with you always 'til the end of the age."[56]

Pentland understands his call as a commissioning to be apostle to contemporary culture. There is good biblical precedent for that. But the aspiration to reclaim some of the denomination's lost cultural influence and the desire

---

55. See Charles Taylor, "Afterword," in Warner, VanAntwerpen, and Calhoun, *Varieties of Secularism*, 318.

56. Pentland, *Fishing Tips*, 216.

## CHAPTER 3. EMBRACING THE CULTURE'S STORIES

to have a lineup outside on Sunday mornings speak of a longing to be loved by the culture, and they make it more difficult for the church to engage critically with the culture and with other faith and belief positions. Pentland is motivated by a desire for the church to be a force for good and a prophetic voice, but a clear priority for him is to be in, and of, the world and a key participant in the cultural conversation. The desire to be relevant comes at a cost, however: creeds, dogma, doctrine, language, and many traditional practices of the church are jettisoned or modified almost beyond recognition in order to facilitate connection to contemporary culture. A case might be made that this is an appropriate strategy of evangelism, indigenizing the gospel and church traditions for a secular age. The numbers prove that it has been a successful growth strategy for Hillhurst.

What seems absent from this particular effort at evangelism are the recognizable contours of the story at the heart of our faith: the story of the life, death, and resurrection of Jesus Christ. Pentland celebrates Bass's reversal of the *believe—behave—belong* triad to *belong—behave—believe* because he is convinced that belief is the wrong place to start, and that creating the conditions for belonging is the appropriate first step. But belonging is only a first step. It is meant to be a step that leads in a direction towards belief, in a process akin to the conversion of which Taylor writes. In Pentland's case, it is not clear what the content of the evangelistic message is, other than a warm and hospitable welcome into a community that will explore questions of meaning loosely guided by an understanding of Jesus primarily as a teacher of timeless truths. That in itself is not a bad thing; clearly many people have responded positively to the invitation and *Fishing Tips* documents numerous testimonies to the sustaining and enriching power of participation in the Hillhurst community. In the closing pages of the book, Pentland muses about the future of the denomination and considers the "things that unite us—spiritual Laws that undergird all life, spiritual practices, the Lord's Prayer, our Creed, and concern for social and humanitarian dimensions of the Gospel, to name a few."[57] I don't know if this list comprises Pentland's inventory of the essentials of the Christian faith, but if it does a question arises: Is it enough? Perhaps Pentland is lining out the contours of a new church for a secular age. But I remain troubled by its resemblance to United Church congregations of the Christendom era—embedded in culture, popular and successful, demographically diverse—and theologically compromised. Could it be that in reacting so strongly against some of the

---

57. Pentland, *Fishing Tips*, 217.

negative stereotypes of the church of that era—how 'churchy' and traditional it was—Pentland has created a modern mirror image of it?

## 3.4 Conclusion

> A church that cuts itself off from its tradition is a church that has severed itself from the very sources whereby it might be renewed. ... We subtly laid aside the notion of the church as the gathering of those who were trying to follow Jesus and presented the church as a gathering of like-minded people who are seeking to live vaguely better lives, who are committed to certain amorphous values like "justice," or "affirmation," or whatever else the culture happened to be infatuated with at that moment.[58]

In this reflection on the preaching of the mainline Protestant church of the 1960s, William H. Willimon points to the dangers inherent in forging too close a bond between the church and culture, and draws our attention to the critical importance of tradition. The church is called to witness to the culture and, as Barth's story of the Bible and the newspaper attests, the gospel is always inherently relevant to every human culture. Our task is to make those connections, which is what Pentland is aiming to do at Hillhurst. But—and here Barth supplies the critical detail—it is the gospel and its story of the life, death, and resurrection of Jesus Christ that enables us to interpret the world, and not vice versa. The gospel, and this story, supplies the core content for Christian meditation on questions of meaning.

When this story is seen as unbelievable, unsupportable within the framework of modernity, it gets cut down, truncated, to fit within a closed, immanent frame. When this story is reduced to the meanings available within the immanent frame—that Jesus is a teacher of good ethical principles that accord with the modern moral order—it is drained of its salvific power. It may still make a difference in the lives of people who are inspired by the teachings of Jesus to live somewhat better lives, and that is a positive outcome. But it leaves us essentially on our own in the universe. The line between the gospel and culture, and between the church and the world, cannot simply be erased, except by renouncing the possibility of transcendence.

---

58. Willimon, "Up from Liberalism," in Copenhaver, Robinson, and Willimon, *Good News in Exile*, 29–30.

## CHAPTER 3. EMBRACING THE CULTURE'S STORIES

Our next chapter will critically examine a proposal for the future of the United Church that makes precisely this assertion: that we are on our own in the universe, without access to the God of the Christian tradition. We turn now to an examination of Gretta Vosper's call for an atheist church.

# Chapter 4. Writing God Out of the Story

To be Christian is not to say specific words, attend a particular church, believe in a certain set of doctrinal beliefs, or participate in a special ritual; indeed these things would be anathema to an individual who was trying to get people to see and live with deep respect for one another's humanity. To be Christian, for me, is to do whatever it takes to bind me to a life lived in a radically ethical way.

—Gretta Vosper, *With or Without God*[1]

When one gives up Christian belief one thereby deprives oneself of the *right* to Christian morality.... Christianity is a system, a consistently thought out and *complete* view of things. If one breaks out of it a fundamental idea, the belief in God, one thereby breaks the whole thing to pieces: one has nothing of any consequence left in one's hands.... Christian morality is a command: its origin is transcendental ... it possesses truth only if God is truth—it stands or falls with the belief in God.

—Friedrich Nietzsche, *Twilight of the Idols*[2]

Gretta Vosper is a phenomenon. Ordained to ministry in the United Church of Canada in 1992, Vosper currently describes herself on her website as "minister, author, atheist," and notes that "for the most part, my denomination—one I consider to be the most progressive in the world—tolerates me as I continue to irritate it toward publicly stating what so many who lead within it believe: god is a metaphor for goodness and love lived out

---

1. Vosper, *With or Without*, 197.
2. Friedrich Nietzsche, *Twilight of the Idols*, 81.

with compassion and justice, no more and no less."[3] She makes the further claim in her website biography—perhaps with a hint of pride—that "twice, I have narrowly avoided heresy trials, once by a margin of three votes" and describes a current process undertaken by the denomination to determine her effectiveness as a minister, a process which could result in Vosper's removal from United Church ministry and dismissal from her current congregation. On the same page, she notes the publication of her two books—the bestselling *With or Without God* in 2008 and *Amen* in 2012—and describes her numerous speaking engagements, media appearances, and the attention her work receives in the monthly denominational magazine, *The United Church Observer*, and on social media.[4] A search on *The Observer*'s website revealed almost forty articles about or by Vosper in the past decade, and letters in reference to Vosper, her ministry, or the current review process appear frequently in the letters section of the magazine.[5] A Google search for "Gretta Vosper" yields over twenty thousand results and reveals coverage from most leading Canadian media outlets, including newspapers, magazines, radio, and television. Stories about Vosper have appeared in *The Guardian*, *Huffington Post*, and *Christianity Today*.[6] Gretta Vosper is arguably the single most well-known minister in the United Church of Canada today; her celebrity as an atheist minister makes her perhaps the most polarizing figure in the denomination as well.

In the foreword to Vosper's first book, *With Or Without God: Why the Way We Live is More Important Than What We Believe*, retired Episcopal

---

3. Vosper, "Little Bit About Me."

4. Vosper, "Little Bit About Me."

5. Of the eleven issues published in the past year, every one contained at least two letters about Vosper, with some issues featuring eight or nine letters. A total of forty-nine letters were published in the course of the year, with about 60 percent of those expressing support or sympathy for Vosper. It must be noted that this letter count may not constitute an accurate reflection of the sentiment in the church. In response to my enquiry, *Observer* editor David Wilson suggested that the overall balance of letters received by the magazine has been fairly evenly split between those sympathetic or supportive of Vosper and those who are critical.

6. Ashifa Kassam, "Atheist Pastor Sparks Debate by 'Irritating the Church into the 21st Century,'" *The Guardian*, April 24, 2016, https://www.theguardian.com/world/2016/apr/24/atheist-pastor-canada-gretta-vosper-united-church-canada; Ryan J. Bell, "A Year Without God Becomes Life After God," *Huffington Post*, September 2, 2015, http://www.huffingtonpost.com/ryan-j-bell/year-without-god_b_8071974.html; Lucinda Borkett-Jones, "Atheist Church Minister Being Reviewed for Her 'Effectiveness,'" *Christianity Today*, June 3, 2015, http://www.christiantoday.com/article/atheist.church.minister.being.reviewed.for.her.effectiveness/55317.htm; all items accessed August 16, 2016.

Bishop and writer John Shelby Spong describes her as a rising star in the progressive Christianity movement who is making a courageous stand against traditionalists, evangelicals, and fundamentalists within the denomination: "Her church has a choice to make. It can either follow Gretta's lead and venture into unknown waters or it can begin the process of marginalizing her. What remains certain is that, with the publication of this book, nothing will ever be the same, not for Gretta, nor for The United Church of Canada, perhaps not even for Christianity."[7] In contrast to Bishop Spong's effusive praise and generous assessment of Vosper's importance for the future of the church, newspaper columnist Douglas Todd offers a more tepid appraisal, describing her as "semi-famous" and noting that "it is not a put-down to suggest if Vosper was not writing and speaking about her atheism from an ostensibly Christian pulpit she would be widely ignored."[8]

Despite the diversity of views, what remains true is that Vosper is a uniquely influential presence in the United Church of Canada today and it is for this reason that we will undertake a critical examination of her proposals for the church and the beliefs that underlie them. I will follow the same pattern I used in the previous chapter, beginning with a summary of Vosper's key ideas and following with a critical examination using the four themes derived from Charles Taylor's work in *A Secular Age*.

## 4.1 Without God

This presentation of Vosper's thought will focus on four major themes: the God she no longer believes in; the God we *must not* believe in, or the dangers inherent in theism; her critique of the liberal church; and her proposal for a post-theistic church. On her website, Vosper traces the development of her identity over a period of fifteen years:

> In 2001, I made it clear that I did not believe in a supernatural, interventionist, divine being. At first, I identified as a non-theist as I do in my first book, *With or Without God*, published in 2008. In my second book, *Amen*, I felt the need to further distinguish myself from those who used the term "non-theist" but retained a belief in the supernatural aspects of god; there, I identified as

---

7. Vosper, *With or Without*, xv.

8. Douglas Todd, "How Do You Solve a Problem Like Gretta Vosper, Atheist Clergywoman?," *Vancouver Sun*, July 5, 2015, accessed August 11, 2016, http://vancouversun.com/news/staff-blogs/how-do-you-solve-a-problem-like-gretta-vosper-atheist-clergy.

## CHAPTER 4. WRITING GOD OUT OF THE STORY

a theological non-realist. In 2013, I embraced the term "atheist" which means, literally, no belief in a theistic, supernatural being.[9]

The notion of development is important, because it enables us to understand Vosper's thinking in continuity with aspects of the Christian tradition. She is not an outsider to the tradition; as we will see, she understands herself and her work as emerging from Christian tradition. Peter Wyatt names this stance as "post-theism": "to be a post-theist rather than an a-theist is to affirm that there is significant continuity between the faith once held and the new stance.... This evolutionary nature of post-theism means that exercising ministry and gathering liturgically are still valued by many non-theists."[10]

Vosper's turn away from traditional theism is rooted in her understanding of modernity, in particular the idea that science makes theistic belief untenable: "simply put, as science has been able to explain more and more of what we experience in the world, God is needed less and less as an explanatory factor."[11] As we have seen, this is part of the standard subtraction story of secularization with which Taylor takes issue. Vosper takes it as gospel, as part of what appears to be a linear read of history as inherently progressive. God's disappearance is understood as a natural development, as part of the evolution of human understanding from a dependent and fearful theistic outlook to a liberated and responsible atheism. Vosper notes the pioneering work of John A. T. Robinson, and cites New Zealand theologian Lloyd Geering as suggesting that "non-theism not only grows out of the Christian tradition but is the only logical next step for the church to take."[12] As with the secular theologians of the 1960s, the focus is on a transition out of childhood tutelage and into maturity and a responsible, grown-up stance towards the world. Vosper imagines early human prehistory and the challenges of living on a volatile and dangerous planet: "you begin to realize how essential it was to find something that would take care of you, something that would shelter you, something that would keep the reckless writhing of the world at bay."[13] Humans invented God as a security blanket, but as our confidence in our capacities has grown, we have unmasked the

---

9. Vosper, "About," grettavosper.ca, accessed August 16, 2016, http://www.grettavosper.ca/about/.
10. Wyatt, "Post-Theism and the 'Problem' of God," 15.
11. Vosper, *With or Without*, 233.
12. Vosper, *With or Without*, 231.
13. Vosper, *With or Without*, 67.

illusions of Oz and come to understand "that like Dorothy, we need to make it work ourselves."[14] Making it work and taking responsibility for ourselves involves two steps, one negative and one positive. Negatively, we recognize "that there are no supernatural beings, forces, or energies necessary for or even mindful of our survival"; positively, "we are our creators, and we have the challenge before us to create a future for this planet in which love, made incarnate through justice and compassion, is the supreme value."[15] We will return to the positive and creative side of this pair below, but here it is important to note the degree of subjectivity that is involved:

> We get to acknowledge whatever tools have helped us make it this far, and to sort through those tools and choose which ones we're going to need for the next leg of the journey. Which experiences from the past will help us shift out of the conundrums we currently experience—personally, communally, globally? What is worthy of a new tomorrow and what is just baggage?[16]

This shift out of theism is not presented as an option by Vosper, as one possible future orientation that might coexist with other patterns. She sees it as a necessity, something that *must* happen, because of the persistent dangers of theistic belief.

Vosper wants us to understand that theism is not only an outmoded or foolish preference based on childish falsehoods, but that it is actually an *invalid* position. Theism is inextricably linked to violence and other forms of harm inflicted on our fellow human beings, other creatures, and the ecosystem of which we are a part. In the wake of the religiously motivated terror attacks on the offices of *Charlie Hebdo* in Paris in January 2015, Vosper wrote an open letter to United Church Moderator Gary Paterson, criticizing the denomination's prayer response to the attack for affirming "the existence of a supernatural being":

> This belief has led to innumerable tragedies throughout the timeline of human history and will continue to do so until it fades from our ravaged memory. If we maintain that our moral framework is dependent upon that supernatural being, we allow others to make the same claim and must defend their right to do so even if their choices and acts are radically different from our own; we do not

---

14. Vosper, *Amen*, 268.
15. Vosper, *With or Without*, 316.
16. Vosper, *Amen*, 44.

## CHAPTER 4. WRITING GOD OUT OF THE STORY

hold the right to parcel out divine authority only to those with whom we agree.

I urge you to lead our church toward freedom from such idolatrous belief.[17]

Setting aside Vosper's astonishing assertion that classical theism is a form of idolatry, her claim here is that it is not possible to separate a benign variant of theism from a malevolent one. When we allow the claim that "God is on our side," that God approves of our efforts or blesses our course of action, we cannot restrict the ways others perceive God's agency. When we make such claims, we open ourselves to the possibility that others might even weaponize their understanding of God's agency. Vosper also raises the issue of theodicy and the apparent capriciousness of a God who would save some and damn others, as further evidence of the inherent harms of theistic belief: "our Christian belief system reinforces that we, if believers, are privileged, that God is on our side, that we are saved because God loves us better than whoever that other poor wretch may have been."[18] Central to Vosper's concern is her belief that "religion, by its very nature, is divisive. Its rituals, traditions, the things it calls sacred become tools that work to identify tribe and distinguish clan."[19] Her rejection of theism is motivated by a quest for universal values that undergird peaceful coexistence amongst all peoples, creatures, and the ecosystem.

Vosper also understands the persistence of theistic belief to be disempowering, undermining the hard-won achievements of human intellectual and technological development. The rituals and traditions of the Christian faith—particularly the practice of prayer and the central place accorded to Scripture—are, at best, unnecessarily limiting of human potential and, at worst, downright abusive:

We need language that will challenge us to get up from our knees, hand us back our dignity, ignite our compassion, and help us to find all those crucial ways we need to live love into the world. Language that reinforces a system of belief that can drive someone back down to his knees, remove his dignity, hold him to a standard he can never meet, and silence his objection to the way things are

---

17. Vosper, "A Letter to Gary Paterson Regarding Paris," grettavosper.ca, accessed August 11, 2016, http://www.grettavosper.ca/letter-gary-paterson-regarding-paris/.
18. Vosper, *With or Without*, 29.
19. Vosper, *With or Without*, 148.

with the promise of something no one has the right to promise unless she also has the power to bring it about is repugnant.[20]

Here Vosper is expressing her concern with the way Christian teaching about prayer and the afterlife can anesthetize believers. Vosper also finds it necessary to delegitimize the Bible as sacred Scripture and to neutralize the divine status of Jesus. She creates a disparaging acronym for the Bible—TAWOGFAT (the authoritative word of God for all time)[21]—and suggests that "we place the book on our shelf with all the other interesting books that we look to for insight and enjoyment and challenge."[22] For Vosper, the Bible—like God—has outlived its usefulness: "we will continue, we must continue, to discern our way forward toward ethical living quite apart from the Bible as we have learned to do. The Bible can no longer assist us in that endeavour."[23] Pointing out that rejecting traditional theism necessarily resolves the question of Jesus' divinity,[24] Vosper invites us to question whether Jesus is such a good role model in any case: "He is not recorded as having attempted to change any oppressive forces, but taught people rather to acquiesce ('turn the other cheek')—a stance that is fine to a point but not at all helpful in ending slavery, racism, patriarchal hierarchy, and so on."[25] At another point, Vosper acknowledges Jesus' "challenges to the status quo, his recognition of brokenness, and his upholding of the oppressed," but sees these as values that are incarnated by "any number of social-justice heroes and spiritual leaders," and may be incarnated by anyone.[26] Vosper's relativization of the Bible and of Jesus continues the theme of subjectivity noted above. The Bible and Jesus are no longer authoritative for us; now we judge Scripture and Jesus by criteria we have determined: "the question to bring to any of the stories of the Bible, once we no longer see it as TAWOGFAT, is: What do you make of it? not What is the meaning of the story? *You* bring the meaning to it. It's not there without you reading it and getting something out of it."[27]

---

20. Vosper, *Amen*, 203.
21. Vosper, *With or Without*, 53.
22. Vosper, *With or Without*, 221.
23. Vosper, *With or Without*, 222.
24. Vosper, *With or Without*, 237.
25. Vosper, *With or Without*, 242.
26. Vosper, *With or Without*, 249.
27. Vosper, *With or Without*, 222.

## CHAPTER 4. WRITING GOD OUT OF THE STORY

Vosper's subjective approach to God, the Bible, and Jesus echoes the perspective of secularist critics of the 1960s. Just as Robinson and Berton had demanded that the church subject its stories to the tests of relevance and credibility, so Vosper insists "rational questions *must* be brought to the stories we read in the Bible precisely because those stories don't make sense. From the very first page to the last one, we keep running across things that tax the credulity of most rational people."[28] In continuity with her secularist forebears of half a century ago, Vosper is intent on pushing the liberal church to say what it means and mean what it says. She is unrelenting in her critique of the liberal church's complacency, its imprecision as to beliefs, and its desire to please everyone and offend no one. Again tracing her development as a leader, Vosper confesses, "I write as a minister who has moved from the centre of liberal Christian thought to the bleeding edge of Christianity, struck by the complacency with which I had accepted the liberal framework and shamed by it as well."[29] She attributes the decline in liberal mainline denominations to "their refusal to state what they actually believe," leading some to exit for conservative denominations that offer more clearly defined beliefs, while others wander off into self-directed spiritual pursuits.[30] Vosper describes the United Church's 1968 "A New Creed" as an initiative that "allowed those in the church who were questioning some of the traditional beliefs of the Christian church to remain within the embrace of the United Church."[31] She sees this as part of the liberal church's determination to stay in a muddy middle ground theologically speaking, and she refuses to let the church off the hook.

What is at stake for Vosper in this is maintaining her insistence that there can be no distinction between benign forms of theism and malevolent ones. So, while liberal Christians may insist on reading the Bible metaphorically and developing images for God that soften or negate attributes that seem indefensible to modern liberal pluralist ears, Vosper remains unconvinced. Citing the work of Marcus Borg and his commitment to the project of translating the traditions, rituals, stories, and language of the church into a liberal conceptual framework, Vosper questions the utility of this approach:

---

28. Vosper, *With or Without*, 220.
29. Vosper, *With or Without*, 15.
30. Vosper, *With or Without*, 45.
31. Vosper, *With or Without*, 97.

> So "Jesus is Lord" really means "love is supreme." Well, then why not say "love is supreme"? All the world can understand that. They can embrace it regardless of their beliefs. If "Jesus is Lord" means "justice for all," then let's say that. Is it that we feel we need "theospeak," theological code words, to keep us connected to our heritage? They will surely do that but beware; "Jesus is Lord" is connected to our *entire* heritage, the full scope of proselytization, dogmatism, exclusivity, condemnation, and violence.[32]

The project of translation cannot work for Vosper because even as liberal Christians might change the meaning of the words inherited from the tradition, the meaning of these words remains unchanged for evangelical and fundamentalist Christians and in the public imagination. Vosper is particularly critical of liberal attempts to develop more palatable descriptive language and imagery for God. Here she makes a compelling counterargument to liberal critics who accuse atheists of straw man arguments:

> Some liberal colleagues, usually those who identify themselves as progressive, argue that the god I have been talking about—the authoritarian, judgmental, capricious, up-in-the-sky god we've called "God" lo these many years—is not the god they bow their heads before. Their beliefs are more sophisticated than that, they say. In fact, they tell me, their god isn't a being that lives in *any* elsewhere, not just up in the sky. The god they believe in is less being-ish, less angry-ish, less authoritarian-ish. And it's not supernatural either. Or omnipotent. Or omnipresent. It's more a "not this" and a "not that" kind of god.[33]

Vosper appears to be describing process theology and panentheism here, and her identification of this as a common theological position in the liberal church appears to be borne out by a recent survey. United Church minister Richard Bott was inspired to undertake a survey of the beliefs of his fellow ministers after watching an interview with Vosper in which she claimed that "it would be at least upwards of 50% of the clergy in the United Church who don't believe in a theistic, supernatural, God."[34] In the survey, approximately 80 percent of respondents indicated that they would not include themselves in the "upwards of 50%" figure Vosper had suggested. Almost 95 percent indicated some form of belief in God, with the largest

---

32. Vosper, *With or Without*, 118.
33. Vosper, *Amen*, 169.
34. Bott, "Preliminary Report," 2.

## CHAPTER 4. WRITING GOD OUT OF THE STORY

single group—at 51.3 percent—choosing panentheism as the option closest to their understanding of God.[35]

Vosper sees this choice as a fudge: "liberal theologies are high on poetry and low on clarity, and we need to ask what that is about."[36] She extends this critique to the liturgy of liberal churches, suggesting that liturgical practices are fundamentally dishonest, either out of clergy leaders's deference to the comfort of participants or out of unexamined habit: "there are those who are happy to assert agreement with the scholarship that clearly exposes the Bible, Christianity, the concept of Christ, Jesus' divinity, and so on as human constructs, yet who demand clergy remain committed to language that claims otherwise."[37] In the liberal church, liturgical habits are maintained even while their meaning is lost:

> The benevolence of a divine being, the beautiful relationship we could have with it, the props and punchlines of children's talks and lectionary illustrations—all felt so normal and right in the context of congregational ministry. . . . We don't think about what our words and actions really mean. (What does it mean to say a commendation at the end of a funeral? What happens when we place water on a child's head during a baptism? What are we implying when we smudge a bit of ash on someone's forehead?)[38]

Vosper is describing a church that has forgotten its story, and she exposes the hollowness of such a project. Based on my experience in leadership in the United Church over the past decade, I think this is an accurate assessment of much liturgical practice in our denomination. Our liturgies live in a state of limbo: we have rejected, or at least distanced ourselves, from traditional meanings of sacramental and quasi-sacramental practices, enabling us to be clearer about what we do not believe than about what we do believe. At a funeral, we affirm the comforting notion that the departed is smiling down on us from heaven; we are inclined to focus on Communion as a form of mealtime fellowship, and Baptism as a rite of welcome into the family; and many United Church congregations steer well-clear of penitential seasons and practices. All of these may be defensible belief positions within the wider Christian tradition, but the point is that we generally are not able to articulate such a defense and our practices have

---

35. Bott, "Preliminary Report," 6.
36. Vosper, *Amen*, 173.
37. Vosper, *With or Without*, 190.
38. Vosper, *Amen*, 162.

come untethered from their meaning. Our liturgies have become zombie liturgies, lurching ever onward in the same basic form but without a living, animating spirit. Vosper is calling time on the zombie liberal church and challenging it to be reborn in a new form.

## 4.2 A Post-Theistic Church

Having reviewed Vosper's rejection of classical theism and her critique of the liberal church, we turn now to the constructive side of her project, her vision for a post-theistic church. Vosper enters into this discussion by posing the obvious question: why bother?[39] If God is dead, the Bible is of questionable utility and the man Jesus has a poor track record when it comes to social justice action—and if, on top of all that, liturgies have become empty ritual—why bother indeed? Further, "if social issues and personal life transitions are adequately covered by secular organizations, then what's the use of church?"[40] Surely the day of the church is done. But Vosper sees life in the old institution still, and she wants to harness it for new—or renewed—purposes: "I do find it hard to imagine that preserving an institution for preservation's sake itself is anything more than an enormous waste of time and energy. But I do think that the church is well placed to bring about some significant change in the world."[41] She continues: "no other organization has that networking ability. No other organization has that kind of access to adults, many of whom are quite prepared to change their lifestyle if it is going to positively impact the world."[42] Like a savvy executive plotting a hostile takeover, Vosper has a keen appreciation for the liberal church's assets. The key asset for Vosper is the liberal church's progressive theology, rooted in the liberal theological tradition:

> The church we need to create will move forward without the negative trappings it has dragged with it from our distant, fearful past. The liberal church, unlike the evangelical church, has in hand the single most important tool needed to do just that. It has been the womb of critical contemporary scholarship for decades. Without being open to that scholarship, without carefully excising the supernatural from its beliefs, without staking more import in this

39. Vosper, *With or Without*, 283.
40. Vosper, *With or Without*, 284.
41. Vosper, *With or Without*, 284.
42. Vosper, *With or Without*, 285.

## CHAPTER 4. WRITING GOD OUT OF THE STORY

world than the next, no church will ever help humanity ably deal with the issues facing it now.[43]

Vosper expresses a concern that lest the church "speak clearly and truthfully about the Bible, about Jesus, about the cross, it will slowly disconnect itself from what might have been its strongest asset."[44] Returning to the baby and the bathwater analogy raised in our discussion of John Pentland in the previous chapter, we again ask which is which? Vosper is proposing that the church disconnect itself from traditional teachings about the Bible, about Jesus, and about the cross—the very things that are surely the church's greatest assets, certainly more so than the modern critical scholarship on the Bible, Jesus, and the cross.

Vosper foresees that "the work of transforming a religious institution, congregation by congregation, from a religious activity-focused community to a sacred-values or humanitarian or eco-centric spiritual community is unfathomable,"[45] and she calls on the denomination to offer support to leaders as they "recreate what it means to be a church and develop new 'atheologies' and commentaries on virtue instead of on ancient texts and fragments of texts."[46] Vosper imagines churchgoers having to suddenly flee the church's impending ruin—as from a house on fire—and wonders what valued possessions they might snatch from the cataclysm,[47] recalling the theme we have encountered previously of returning to the essential core of Christianity freed from the encrustations of dogma, doctrine, language, and practices. The pipe organ will need to be left behind, as will the Bible.[48] As to deciding what will be taken forward into the church of the future? In keeping with the subjectivity noted above, "the power to find those things, the power to choose them, the power to use them appropriately rests, as it always has, in our hands—only now, we know. It's time we accessed our freedom and took up our responsibility."[49] This is another expression of the growing up and taking responsibility theme that is central to secular theology. Also in keeping with secular theology, as part of the transition to its post-theistic incarnation, the church must learn to speak the language of

43. Vosper, *With or Without*, 306.
44. Vosper, *With or Without*, 307.
45. Vosper, *With or Without*, 289.
46. Vosper, *With or Without*, 275.
47. Vosper, *Amen*, 40.
48. Vosper, *With or Without*, 203.
49. Vosper, *With or Without*, 215.

the world: "if we are to be an influence for good, for comfort, for strength, for growth, we must use the language of those who come to us, not require that they come to understand ours."[50]

While drawing close to the culture through the use of shared language, Vosper's post-theistic church also has a countercultural element. Recalling Flatt's citation of Smith's subcultural identity theory, Vosper acknowledges that "a clear, well-defined identity that sets a group apart from the culture in which it exists will better ensure its survival than a regular influx of lottery winnings."[51] Reflecting on the needs of youth and adults respectively, she queries whether "religion can provide a values-based alternative to what popular culture provides" and affirms that "something or someone needs to apply constant pressure against the values that a consumer society sets as the most desirable."[52] It is, to say the least, unfortunate that Vosper is not able to locate this countercultural, values-based witness in the gospel. Nevertheless her call for a stronger witness in this regard can be read as a critique of the liberal church's cozy accommodation to culture and as a challenge to do better.

At the heart of Vosper's project for a post-theistic church is a set of core values that include: "beauty, forgiveness, delight, love, respect, wisdom, honour, creativity, tranquility, imagination, humour, awe, truth, purity, justice, courage, fun, compassion, challenge, knowledge, and trustworthiness."[53] The purpose of the post-theistic church is to identify and uphold such values as the irreplaceable elements of human cultural heritage, without which human life would be diminished:

> In the postmodern church, we're looking for what our small-g god—the humanly constructed set of life-enhancing values we strive to uphold—challenges us to do. What will bring about the most life-enhancement for all? What leaves the earth best able to heal from our misuse of its resources? What is the choice that manifests the best not only for our time but for generations to come?[54]

In essence, the God of classical theism is replaced by a set of core values that elicit our reverence. The doublespeak of the liberal church, necessitated by its attachment to the language of classical theism, is replaced by clear,

50. Vosper, *With or Without*, 26.
51. Vosper, *Amen*, 39.
52. Vosper, *With or Without*, 100, 101.
53. Vosper, *With or Without*, 216.
54. Vosper, *With or Without*, 281–82.

## CHAPTER 4. WRITING GOD OUT OF THE STORY

universally understood, plain language. Shorn of our childish dependence on an imagined God-in-the-sky who will protect us, and forced to stand up, grow up, and take responsibility for ourselves, the liberal church's complacency is replaced by a newfound sense of commitment and solidarity for our fellow human beings and the entire creation. Despite her own strong criticism of the liberal church's "comfortable pews," Vosper sees the possibility of redeeming this perceived failure as a *charism* instead:

> Mainline denominations have often been criticized from both evangelical and sacramental perspectives for being nothing more than "clubs," places where people go to meet like-minded people, perhaps commit to some shared values, and enjoy one another's company. Perhaps that isn't a criticism after all. Perhaps community is exactly and only what we need to be.[55]

Such is the post-theistic church of Vosper's vision. In her words, "it is simply the best of what is left when liberal Christians clear their desks of what they no longer believe of the Christian message."[56] In Taylor's terms, this is a classic subtraction story.

In a passage that recalls Berton's "general principles" of Christianity that we encountered in chapter 1—"truth is better than a lie, honesty better than a deceit, love and mercy better than hate and mistrust"[57]—Vosper writes, "couldn't the church, especially the liberal church—with its heritage of critical scholarship and passion for social justice—strike out boldly and proclaim that life is real and love is good and everything else is just stuff we've created to help us deal with life lovingly?"[58] Secular theology is perennially in search of core values or the general principles of Christianity, out of which it hopes to construct reinvigorated communities of faith. Thus far, a reinvigorated liberal or progressive Christianity has not emerged, suggesting that shared values may not be enough to sustain a community of countercultural witness.

In summary, this presentation of Vosper's thought has focused on four themes: her understanding of theism as incompatible with modernity; the dangers inherent in theism; her critique of the liberal church; and her proposal for a post-theistic church. Before turning to a critical examination of Vosper's ideas in light of our four themes from Taylor, we will take a closer

---

55. Vosper, *With or Without*, 309–10.
56. Vosper, *With or Without*, 311.
57. Berton, *Comfortable Pew*, 113.
58. Vosper, *Amen*, 191.

look at one additional element of Vosper's thought—her understanding of transcendence—as this plays a key role in Taylor's story.

## 4.3 Transcendence, Immanence, and "Transimmanence"

An important concept in the work of Charles Taylor is *transcendence*. In the opening pages of *A Secular Age*, Taylor offers a three-dimensional definition:

> A possibility of transformation is offered, which takes us beyond merely human perfection. But of course, this notion of a higher good as attainable by us could only make sense in the context of belief in a higher power, the transcendent God of faith which appears in most definitions of religion. But then thirdly, the Christian story of our potential transformation by agape requires that we see our life as going beyond the bounds of its "natural" scope between birth and death; our lives extend beyond "this life."[59]

Taylor's definition rests upon an acknowledgement of the reality of the existence of God. It is our relationship with God that enables us to see beyond the aspiration to flourishing or fulfillment in our natural lives, and to be willing to spend ourselves in the service of others. Citing the work of Luc Ferry, Taylor acknowledges a form of self-transcendence that yet remains immanent, a "horizontal" rather than a "vertical" transcendence.[60] Taylor concludes that such forms of immanent transcendence, based on appeals to shared values and altruism, are insufficient to motivate sustained transformative behavior. In a document prepared for the committee conducting the current review into her effectiveness as a minister, Vosper cites the work of Philip Goldberg and his "five significant tasks of religion." The fifth task is *transcendence*, which

> provides a reference point beyond the individual or community which challenges them to expand their understanding to experience themselves as integrated within a larger whole, the web of life. This can be understood as the realization of the impact one has on the vast expanse of life both during and beyond his or her lifetime and does not require belief in a supernatural realm.[61]

---

59. Taylor, *Secular Age*, 20.
60. Taylor, *Secular Age*, 677.
61. Vosper, "My Answers to the Questions of Ordination."

This definition does include Taylor's criteria of a perspective beyond one's natural life, but clearly lacks the criteria of a relationship with God that leads one "beyond merely human perfection." It comes closer to the perspective of Ferry and the notion of horizontal transcendence. In *Amen*, Vosper coins a new term—"transimmanence"—to describe the sense of an immanent self-transcendence: "we need what is outside of us—beyond us—too, intermingling it with what is within—a transimmanence that has been the source of all the good we have experienced, whether we've attributed it to something supernatural or simply the normal unfolding of life."[62] Vosper makes clear that going beyond does not entail acknowledgement of a supernatural realm, but rather "the natural world, including all the things about it we cannot explain,"[63] as well as our relationships with others.

## 4.4 Charles Taylor in Dialogue with Gretta Vosper

As we did in the previous chapter, we turn now to the four themes drawn from the work of Charles Taylor in *A Secular Age*. These four themes will supply a template to guide our evaluation of Gretta Vosper's proposal for a post-theistic church. The four themes are: 1) Taylor's "correction" of the standard secularization thesis, including his refutation of its basic premise of inexorability and the narrative of subtraction; 2) the identification of secularity with a mature, responsible, "grown up" stance towards the world and the divine; 3) Taylor's positive assessment of the spirituality of the quest, and the opportunities for engagement it suggests; and 4) Taylor's suggestions for the role of orthodox expressions of faith in the context of pluralism.

Taylor's main thesis is the rejection of the standard subtraction account of secularization which reads history in a linear, progressive fashion: over the centuries as North Atlantic civilization has modernized, the realm of science and the rational must increase and the dominion of the religious must decrease. Yet it is this very premise that is foundational to Vosper's work. As we have seen, she makes the claim that the scientific account of reality has displaced the previous theological account. The inevitability that Vosper reads in Geering's prediction that non-theism is "the only logical next step for the church to take"[64] and her assertion that the post-theistic

---

62. Vosper, *Amen*, 212.
63. Vosper, *Amen*, 215.
64. Vosper, *With or Without*, 233.

church is "simply the best of what is left"[65] when liberal Christians clear away the detritus of dogma and tradition also depend on this linear read of the advance of secularization. In contrast, Taylor shows that modernity does not inexorably lead to the diminishment of religion, although it profoundly shapes its forms and presentation. For Taylor, religion is perennially and persistently adapting and responding to its cultural context. At times those adaptations do not reflect the best of the Christian message; at times they have a negative impact on human flourishing: such is often the impact of the immanent frame. But religion and modernity continuously intersect one another, influencing and fragilizing each other.

Whereas Taylor's nuanced read of the rise of exclusive humanism in the context of the immanent frame is tinged with an awareness of what is lost—diminished reference to the transcendent leads to a sense of the sterility of life, engendering malaise—for Vosper the advance of modernity towards a form of exclusive humanism is something to be celebrated. She sees nothing but sunny uplands as we step out of the dark night of primal, fearful, dependent reliance on the gods of our own conjuring and into the clear daylight of hard-won moral, intellectual, and spiritual freedom. This is our second theme from Taylor: the theme of growing up and taking responsibility that is central to secular theology. Vosper has a profound and abiding confidence in human nature and human potential. This is reflected in her single-minded determination to take hold of the reins and fashion a suitable replacement for the God of classical theism out of a set of core values. Vosper's demotion of God, the Bible, and Jesus is motivated by her commitment to the affirmation of human nature. She sees these core elements of the Christian tradition as contributing to a disfiguring and diminishment of human life and is compelled to cast them aside in order to set free all that is good within us. On this read of the Christian tradition, Vosper's move makes sense. Indeed, Taylor also acknowledges an element of harm and the disfigurement of the *Imago Dei* that result from the rigors of Reform and life in the immanent frame. For Taylor, however, the problem is not inherent to God, the Bible, or Jesus, but instead is a consequence of our human fetishization of control. Vosper and Taylor are in opposing positions here: her unqualified affirmation of the inherent goodness of humankind left to its own devices runs counter to his more qualified view, that normal human drives—like the need for order—can go into overdrive and cause harm.

If you want to see what humans are capable of, Taylor says, look at one of the most astonishing creations of the last millennium—the immanent

---

65. Vosper, *With or Without*, 311.

## CHAPTER 4. WRITING GOD OUT OF THE STORY

frame. Taylor is at pains to affirm human capability and creativity, describing the construction of the immanent frame as a breathtaking achievement with a number of positive consequences. It also, however, has serious limitations. Draw the frame too tightly, and it is as if we are living underground: we become pale and stunted, diminished, when we are cut off from fresh air, sunlight, and room to move. The antidote to life in the immanent frame is maintaining an open window onto transcendence—and not the kind of horizontal transcendence and appeal to altruism that Vosper invokes. For Taylor, that is simply not enough. Our human nature is not enough to save us; only the *Imago Dei* within us can do that: "perhaps only God, and to some extent those who commit themselves to God, can love human beings when they are utterly abject."[66]

Our third theme from Taylor—the spirituality of the quest—reflects a restlessness with life in the immanent frame and the search for something more. As we have seen, Taylor calls for communities of faith to have a stance of hospitality towards questers, inviting them to participate in a journey that includes the possibility of conversion and a relationship to the transcendent. In a manner that strongly echoes the analysis of Cox, Berton, and the secularists of the 1960s, Vosper's unsparing, at times scathing, critique of the liberal church enumerates the various ways this expression of Christianity is failing to live up to its call. The liberal church's complacency, its inability to articulate what it believes, and its desire to please severely compromise its witness and limit its utility as a force for good. As a result people have headed for the exits, seeking the relative certainty provided by evangelical or fundamentalist forms of Christianity or wandering off on a variety of personal spiritual quests. It is the latter group that Vosper wants the liberal church to provide a home for. She calls for a church that is a countercultural witness, challenging the ethic of consumerism and offering life-giving narratives to counter those of popular culture. Her project is built upon a foundation of shared humanist values, and thus requires the abandonment of much of what has been central to the Christian tradition and ecclesiology. To a very large degree, I believe Vosper's analysis is correct—that the liberal church has become neither fish nor fowl and is failing as a communal witness to the gospel—and her proposal for a rebirth of the church as a post-theistic community seeking the transformation of the world is compelling. But, as with Pentland's proposal, it fails Taylor's criteria by remaining closed to the possibility of transcendence. In Vosper's case this is made abundantly clear by her repeated assertions that our fate is in our own hands. Again, as

66. Taylor, *Secular Age*, 684.

with Pentland's proposal, Vosper's post-theistic church may achieve a lot of good and may make a positive difference in many people's lives. It also may prove popular—though I do not see the evidence for that. The congregation Vosper serves—West Hill United Church in Toronto—saw its weekly attendance drop from 125 to 40 after a controversial decision to remove the Lord's Prayer from worship in 2003; after the publication of her books drew attention to her work, attendance has rebounded to 90.[67]

Vosper's dream of transforming the liberal progressive church into the post-theistic church of the future is also a response to the questions raised in our fourth theme from Taylor, the challenge of maintaining a particular faith perspective in the context of a pluralistic, cross-pressured culture. Vosper clearly believes that maintaining a particular faith perspective is neither desirable nor defensible. She sees religious particularity as a source of violence and various other forms of harm, and she comprehensively rejects the liberal church's assertion that a kinder, gentler version of theistic belief is possible. Religion is inherently divisive, and beliefs and dogma only serve to determine and defend the boundaries of the tribe. When asked why she chooses to remain within the United Church of Canada rather than associate with a secular, humanist organization, Vosper turns prophetic, indicating a call to "irritate" the entire denomination into a post-theistic future:

> I want the United Church to accept that the Bible is not the authoritative word of God and that God is not where moral authority resides, and to recognize the innumerable divisions religion has created across millennia. If they had the fortitude to say that, I think it could change the conversation of religion around the world. And that's what I'm betting on.[68]

The subtitle of her first book—"why the way we live is more important than what we believe"—provides a succinct statement of the nature of her project. She is seeking to build some form of spiritual community based on a

---

67. Amy Dempsey, "Meet the United Church Minister Who Came Out as an Atheist," *Toronto Star*, February 21, 2016, accessed August 19, 2016, https://www.thestar.com/news/insight/2016/02/21/meet-the-united-church-minister-who-came-out-as-an-atheist.html. Official statistics from the United Church Year Book tell a slightly different story, showing that weekly attendance remained steady at about 150 for the period 1998–2006 (Vosper was called to the congregation in 1997), before slowly and steadily declining to about 70 for the period 2013–2015.

68. Malcolm Johnston, "Q&A: Gretta Vosper, the United Church Minister Who Doesn't Believe in God," *Toronto Life*, November 25, 2015, accessed August 19. 2016, http://torontolife.com/city/life/gretta-vosper-united-church-minister/.

commitment to shared, universal values, values that are common to a wide range of enduring religious traditions. This is an approach that seeks to resolve the tension of pluralism by erasing all particularity and permitting only those values, beliefs, and practices that everyone can agree on. It is much like saying that languages are inherently divisive, and so we must stop speaking our own ancestral tongues and all learn Esperanto.

Vosper is clearly driven by a desire to disarm the religiously motivated violence that has become a commonplace in our world, along with the abuses of religious practice and belief that have led to the exclusion or denigration of women, LGBTQ persons, people of color, and others. She is right to be concerned about these injustices and wrongs, and to be inspired to change them. Her error lies in an overly simplistic connection between theistic belief and violence and mistreatment. As an atheist who sees more harm than good in religious traditions, it is all too easy for Vosper to make religion the scapegoat, assuming that a religionless world would be a haven of compassion, freedom, love, and all things good. Yet the history of the twentieth and early twenty-first centuries provides ample evidence of unimaginable violence committed by state actors inspired by non-religious, even atheistic, ideologies. Exclusion based on race, gender, and sexual identity is as much an issue in the secular sphere as in the religious one.

Taylor's work demonstrates that erasing religious difference is neither possible nor desirable. Even in our secular age, the world is in many ways becoming more religious. What he proposes instead is respectful dialogue amongst a wide variety of positions including both theistic and atheistic approaches. Arguing from a theistic position, Taylor sees God, and our implication in a transformative relationship with God, as the best guarantor of our humane behavior.

## 4.5 Conclusion

> Should Christian faith be defined by the present feelings of members of the contemporary church? Does the community form Christian faith, or is the church called out from society to be something that it did not (and does not) invent? Can we really "reinvent" Christianity?
>
> —Edwin Searcy[69]

---

69. Searcy, "Making Progress?" 13.

Our discussion of Vosper and her proposal for a post-theistic church inspires questions such as those raised here by Edwin Searcy. A key element of Vosper's approach is what I have referred to as subjectivity: our right, as church members, to define the parameters of faith. Such a view is only possible when transcendence has been eclipsed and we believe ourselves to be firmly locked into the immanent frame. When *we* are all there is, and the God of classical theism is exposed as a vain imagining, a post-theistic church makes sense as an effort to manage human instincts toward productive and hopefully life-enhancing behaviors in community. It is Reform by another name, only now it has become untethered, cut loose from the traditions that have nurtured life in Christian community across two millennia.

We turn now to some further reflections on the future of the United Church of Canada based on our critical examination of the work of Pentland and Vosper.

## Chapter 5. Finding the Heart of the Story

It is necessary to ask, however, whether what remains of *Jesus* in this postreligious, post-Christendom context, can endure. It could be little more than nostalgia, or a convenient stop-gap to cover the repressed atheism and nihilism of those who "mourn the death of God" but are afraid to face the death of meaning that accompanies that 'event'. In order to last beyond the residue of twenty centuries of piety, attention to the Name at the centre must entail some definitive or expectant sense of its significance *pro me, pro nobis*—for me, and for us humans. There must be at least a hint of *indispensability* about it.

—Douglas John Hall, *What Christianity Is Not*[1]

Over the course of the previous two chapters we have reviewed two contemporary expressions of United Church ecclesiology in light of Charles Taylor's story of secularization. The purpose of this review was twofold: first, to show that the proposals of John Pentland and Gretta Vosper—proposals for what the United Church might look like in the twenty-first century—are in historical continuity with the secular theology that swept into the United Church in the 1960s; and second, through the application of Taylor's revision of secularization theory, to question the underlying assumptions of these approaches. My argument to this point has been that the United Church has continued to be strongly influenced by secular theology—and the particular understanding of secularization on which it is based—from the 1960s to the present day, *and* that Taylor's analysis seriously challenges this particular understanding of secularization. What are the implications of Taylor's revised reading of secularization

---

1. Hall, *What Christianity Is Not*, 152.

for the United Church of Canada today and into the future? Should proposals and models built upon foundations that have been "fragilized" by Taylor's critique continue to guide the ecclesiology of the denomination, or is it time to call for new approaches?

The main deficiency our Taylorian review has revealed is that both Pentland's and Vosper's proposals remain firmly within the immanent frame, with a radically narrowed conception of transcendence. For Vosper the window on transcendence is firmly shut: answers may only be sought in the "natural" world; the aspiration to transcendence is redefined, relocated within immanence in her formulation "transimmanence." Pentland suggests something similar in his focus on the horizontal and inner horizons, rather than on the vertical dimension. While Pentland's window may not be as firmly closed as Vosper's, both proposals are grounded in the horizons of the immediate, the here-and-now, and both display a deep skepticism about any reality beyond the immanent. Taylor's thesis suggests that this is to be expected within mainline Christianity after five centuries of Reform, with its hallowing of the secular realm.

Both proposals also attempt to ameliorate the losses that Taylor's thesis describes: the narrowing and truncation of human life in the immanent frame. Pentland and Vosper offer proposals for the renewal of United Church of Canada congregations as institutions, with Pentland offering tips on how congregations might recover lost ground and reclaim a place at the center of public life, while Vosper aims for something akin to a Canadian version of the Sunday Assembly, a secular gathering with roots in the United Kingdom that aims to help people "live better, help often, wonder more."[2] But what are we to make of a church that remains skeptical of, or closed to transcendence, or a church that is no longer able to affirm a belief in the trinitarian God? Or as Douglas John Hall, an ordained United Church of Canada minister and one of North America's preeminent theologians, prompts us to ask in the epigraph that opens this chapter, how long might we expect such institutions to endure without an ability to articulate the indispensable significance of the Name at the heart of our story—Jesus?

This chapter will attempt to address Hall's question by reflecting on the current trajectory of the United Church of Canada as exemplified by the proposals we have been examining. Summarizing the discussion of the previous four chapters, I will bring the work of Pentland and Vosper

---

2. Sunday Assembly, "The Sunday Assembly Motto," sundayassembly.com, accessed August 24, 1016, https://www.sundayassembly.com.

into conversation with the key themes of the 1960s secular theologians and their acolytes, with Taylor, and with the theological insights of Hall in his recent work, *What Christianity Is Not: An Exercise in 'Negative' Theology*. This summary will focus on themes we have been tracing throughout these pages: the critique of the liberal church and its "comfortable pews"; the attempt to retrieve a true, original core of faith unsullied by the accretions of dogma, doctrine, and religion; the motif of growing up and taking responsibility so central to secular theology and its affirmation of human capacity, often expressed in the spirituality of the quest; and the pressing question of pluralism, of discerning the church's relationship to the wider culture, whether to erase the boundaries and blend in or to remain distinctive and, in some sense, countercultural.

My purpose in this chapter will be to focus attention on the limits of some of the approaches of the past half century, and to suggest the outlines of what I believe should be at the heart of the United Church of Canada's story into the future.

## 5.1 The Pews Are Still Too Comfortable

The title of Pierre Berton's 1965 book has become an enduring word image in the Canadian church because these few words manage to say so much, so descriptively, about the perennial challenges of mainline Christianity in this country. Berton and others—such as June Callwood, with her memorable description of the mainline church as a cruise ship lazily plying the waters while neglecting the cries of those who are drowning—captured the sense of the mainline church as primarily inwardly focused, concerned more with the maintenance of its prestige and its facilities than with its gospel calling. On the measures of Cox's key functions of the church—*kerygma* (proclamation), *diakonia* (acts of reconciliation and forms of service), and *koinonia* (communal embodiment of the way of Jesus)—the church of the comfortable pew was seen to be failing dismally. Such churches were shaped and formed more by their heritage and by the cultural norms of their leaders than by the gospel. Yet despite the urgent and insistent calls from critics both outside and within the church for a radical change in orientation— and despite the denomination's robust response—five decades later the comfortable pew appellation remains an apt description of many United Church congregations. Today many congregations are indistinguishable from service clubs, and they face the same demographic challenges as those pillars of social capital—aging members and numerical decline. Each in their own way, the proposals of Pentland and Vosper attempt to respond the malaise of the typical liberal mainline congregation.

Small numbers, aging, and decline characterized the state of the Hillhurst congregation when John Pentland was called to serve as their minister in 2004. Eleven years later Sunday attendance had quadrupled and there were a hundred children in Sunday School as the congregation became generationally diverse and family focused. The congregation's annual budget has increased sevenfold and the numbers of paid staff have multiplied. The key to this transformation, according to Pentland, lay in connecting to the community. Pentland and Hillhurst have enjoyed outstanding success in connecting to the culture through the strategic pursuit of relevance. Popular movies and books are featured in sermons and book discussion groups, and the congregation is attuned to the social, cultural, and political issues that are being talked about in its neighborhood. The result is that, in many ways, Hillhurst resembles a typical United Church of Canada congregation of the post-World War II period. However, if we reflect on "the comfortable pew" critique we can also see some differences. Congregations of the 1960s were castigated for their use of "churchy" or traditional language, and for preaching that failed to engage the quotidian concerns of those in the pews. As we have seen, Pentland eschews "churchy" language, and traditions and practices that might seem alienating or foreign to those Hillhurst is trying to reach. The sacraments and worship services are made accessible by being translated into the language and forms of contemporary culture. Pentland appears to have answered some of the key complaints of the 1960s critics in terms of language, practices, and cultural relevance, and it is clear that Hillhurst has developed into a thriving community. What is less clear is just what kind of community has been formed. For Pentland, being a community that welcomes its neighbors into conversation about life's meaning seems to be enough.

Vosper also sees the formation of community as a worthy goal in itself, as she embraces the liberal church's particular charism of "clubbiness" as a virtue. This is one element of the liberal church tradition that Vosper seeks to preserve even as other elements come in for withering criticism. Like Berton and his colleagues, Vosper punctures the pretensions of the liberal church, exposing the hollowness of its rituals and practices as zombie liturgies whose meaning has been all but lost. Vosper questions the utility of a church that is no longer able to be in integrity with the heritage of

## CHAPTER 5. FINDING THE HEART OF THE STORY

the Christian tradition but remains attached to its forms, hymnody, and language. Her proposed solution is a form of radical honesty in which the church is forced to face its illusions and to choose to leave behind what it can no longer affirm with integrity. What this requires, however, is nothing short of the breathtakingly audacious task of fashioning a replacement for the God of classical theism out of a series of universal and essential shared values. Again we must ask what kind of community results from this radical transplant surgery.

Taylor's thesis suggests that the phenomenon of the comfortable pew, or the inwardly focused church, arises in the context of Reform and the construction of the immanent frame. Specifically, the form of church we know—the form that has been familiar since the time of our great-grandparents—is a product of Taylor's Age of Mobilization. This is a church that had its birth in movements of evangelical social reform: efforts to stamp out drinking and gambling, and to imprint the values of Christendom on the entire social order. Churches in the Age of Mobilization—that is, the old mainline—took on the project of weaving themselves intimately into the social fabric, becoming embedded in their host cultures to the point where so-called Christian values and the marks of good citizenship became indistinguishable. One result of this is that participants in mainline congregations often value the invisibility of their faith, seeing the congruence between their civic religion and the values of the host society as evidence that their form of Christianity is compatible with modernity, and not a threat to the Modern Moral Order—unlike that of evangelicals or fundamentalists. This is a vision of the church not as salt, light, or yeast—holding out to the culture a compelling vision of *koinonia*, what the world would look like if the gospel were lived out—but rather the church as a totalizing enterprise, aiming to gather every last person into its fold. As Taylor points out, the desire to include everyone necessarily means lowering the spiritual bar, so to speak: the value of inclusion means relaxing the standards somewhat. Such a church ends up mirroring the world, replicating and reinforcing its power structures and prejudices. Not only will it fail to help transform the world, it will often actually hinder such transformation.

Taylor's vision of what the church is meant to be is grounded in *agape*, God's unconditional and irrational love for us, and in God's invitation to us to imitate him in expressing this love in community. It is a vision of *koinonia* that disrupts our narrow focus on our own comfort and seeks a broader sharing: a sharing of our comfort with those who are less comfortable, and a willingness to share their discomfort. Taylor warns us of the dangers of institutionalizing *agape*, making it into a program of social service that keeps social barriers and hierarchical distinctions firmly in place; this is a perennial danger for the comfortable pew church. Douglas John Hall offers the story of St. Francis of Assisi as a paradigm of the willingness to accept the disruption of our comfort:

> What the disciple community seeks is to follow, to be obedient to the one who calls it to leave its nets and its preoccupations with self and move out into the world without having to know beforehand that all will be well. In short, to trust. Obedience to this command *may* involve homelessness and hunger and the renunciation of sex, as it did also for Francis; but these are only consequences, *for some*, of following the Christ; they are not of the essence, nor are they intended for all. What *is* mandatory for all who hear this call to discipleship is a transformation of *attitude and orientation*.[3]

Hall's description of communal discipleship here echoes the call of secular theologians in the 1960s for the church to go out and engage the world and—in the words of Phyllis D. Airhart—"to risk theological anonymity and denominational invisibility when they took their faith into the wider community."[4] What seems to have been lost in the intervening decades in United Church congregations is the connection back to the original story, to the gospel and Jesus' call for obedience to this *particular* way of transformation of our attitudes and orientation. The commitment to demonstrating the gospel rather than verbalizing it seems to have opened the way to a diminution of its importance to Christian community. The particular story of the life, death, and resurrection of Jesus Christ has been reduced to a set of general principles or values which are said to derive from the gospels or the teachings of Jesus. This reduction goes hand in hand with a scaling back of *koinonia* and *agape* to the kind of clubby, insider group fellowship that marked the church of the 1950s and 1960s. As a result, the pews are still too comfortable.

## 5.2 Beyond the Lowest Common Denominator

Another theme that has run through the whole length of our story is the attempt to recover a true, original core of Christian belief—the Christianity

---

3. Hall, *What Christianity Is Not*, 120.
4. Airhart, *Church with the Soul of a Nation*, 299.

## CHAPTER 5. FINDING THE HEART OF THE STORY

of Jesus and the earliest church as it were—before it became encased in the creeds, dogmas, doctrines, and practices that have obscured and marred its essential beauty and truth. In the 1960s secularists like Berton spoke of Christianity's "general principles laid down by its founder,"[5] and others suggested that agnostics and atheists might be better Christians than those who wore the label. We saw how the Canadian government in the 1960s fostered the expression of generic Judeo-Christian values as a bulwark of national unity. We have seen how Pentland's rejection of doctrine and dogma, and creeds and practices, is informed by Cox's hypothesis of an original Age of Faith, a pre-creedal expression of Christianity rooted in the early church's experience of Jesus as teacher and healer. Vosper goes even further, questioning the reliability of the gospel's stories of Jesus and relativizing Jesus as one possible exemplar of values that any of us could potentially incarnate. Common to all of these positions are the maxims that—in Vosper's formulation—behavior is more important than belief, and—in Bass's formulation, picked up by Pentland—belonging is more important than belief. These are expressions of the baby and the bathwater trope in which the things we value less (in this case dogmas, doctrines, creeds, and practices) can be profitably cast aside, while those items that we value most (in this case behavior and belonging) are rescued or retrieved.

A question that I have been asking in these pages is whether we have a correct assessment of what is baby and what is bathwater in the church. For what is dispensed with in all that useless dogma and doctrine, creed and practice—what seems to slip down the drain unnoticed—is the question of the divinity of Jesus. Common to all of these positions is serious doubt or outright rejection of this central claim of the church: that Jesus is the Son of God, the second person of the Trinity. Pentland neatly avoids the question, steering clear of the declarative positions of both biblical literalists and atheists. For Vosper the question is resolved by her rejection of theism: no God, so no Son of God.

Whatever struggles we may have with dogmas and doctrines, creeds and practices, they are but the attempts of our forebears to witness to the amazing and unique story at the heart of our faith. In the United Church's history to date four such attempts to articulate our core beliefs have been made: the Twenty Articles of Doctrine in the Basis of Union (1925); A Statement of Faith (1940); A New Creed (1968); and A Song of Faith (2006).[6]

---

5. Berton, *Comfortable Pew*, 113.
6. United Church of Canada, *Manual*, 11–28.

The earliest of these statements affirms "the teaching of the great creeds of the ancient Church" and "our allegiance to the evangelical doctrines of the Reformation."[7] The 1940 statement incorporated elements of the mid-century turn to neo-orthodoxy, while A New Creed bears the hallmarks of the 1960s turn to the secular. The most recent statement, A Song of Faith, attempts to express the traditions of Christian faith in contemporary language and a poetic format. These four statements are recognized as doctrine and—in accordance with the Reformed tradition—as standards subordinate to Scripture.[8] As subordinate standards, each of these statements remains in force as others are adopted, meaning that the collective set of statements are in dialogue with one another. As John H. Young notes,

> doctrine "develops," not in a progressive fashion that judges a current statement better than an older one that should then be left behind, but in the sense that the way we express the faith is always time-conditioned. While a good contemporary statement frames the faith tradition in the context of an era's challenges, it is in the conversation among contemporary statements and those of the historical tradition that both individual and denominational understandings are most enriched.[9]

This is in keeping with Taylor's statement that "our faith is not the acme of Christianity, but nor is it a degenerate version; it should rather be open to a conversation that ranges over the whole of the last 20 centuries (and even in some ways before)."[10] Taylor reminds us of the value of the diverse range of voices across the Christian tradition; our engagement with the whole of the tradition prevents us from making the mistake of assuming that our take on things is inherently superior just because it is the most recent.

Hall likens the development of the church over the centuries to a snowball that started off small and pure but then picked up all sorts of foreign matter as it rolled through the centuries, and invites us to undertake the careful task of teasing apart "the 'kernel' of faith—the *kerygma*—from its cultural accretions."[11] He notes: "no doubt it is impossible at this stage fully to separate the snow from the great variety of stuff picked up along the way,

---

7. United Church of Canada, *Manual*, 11.
8. Young, "What We Say We Believe," 12.
9. Young, "What We Say We Believe," 19.
10. Taylor, *Secular Age*, 754.
11. Hall, *What Christianity Is Not*, 40. When you are Canadian, snow is a natural metaphor!

## CHAPTER 5. FINDING THE HEART OF THE STORY

but the attempt must be made, for much of what was rolled into the huge Christendom snowball is certainly not . . . Christianity!"[12] Like Taylor, Hall recognizes that the church throughout history has contributed to negative stereotypes about doctrine and dogma, and he invites us to recover a sense of doctrine not as a matter of blind assent, but as an expression of faith:

> Doctrine, in the community of faith and in the faithful individual will then not be a discipline of (often reluctant or halfhearted!) assent imposed upon believers by external (or internal!) authority; it will be a necessary, natural, *and joyful*(!) consequence of faith. And because it is the offspring of faith, it will also tolerate faith's opposite—doubt.[13]

The exploration of doctrine within the community of faith must inevitably wrestle with "the figure at the center of its life and its message":

> It is indeed probable that Christianity would not have emerged into history as a distinctive faith had not the early church, pushed by the biblical record, insisted that this "despised and rejected" human being was, *in reality*, far more than a prophet or a failed Messiah. It is also probable that Christianity would cease to be were its adherents no longer prepared to see anything in Jesus beyond that which could be explained in purely human and rational terms.[14]

We see here a recognition that doctrine and dogma and creeds are not the immutable heart of Christian faith; that they are always time- and culture-bound; that they must be tested, and wrestled with, by the individual and in the community—yet they cannot be set aside because they no longer make sense in the terms of our culture and time. Nor can they be reduced to a set of general principles, thus avoiding or ignoring the question of Jesus' divinity. Christian doctrine must wrestle with the figure at the heart of its story.

As we saw with Edwin Searcy's reflections on A New Creed in chapter 1, however, this 1968 statement of faith has become virtually the only creed used regularly in United Church liturgies. Our conversation with the tradition seems to reach no further back than 1968 and we no longer seem able to engage seriously with the church's witness to the divinity of Jesus or other principle doctrines upheld by most Christians in most places in most

---

12. Hall, *What Christianity Is Not*, 40.
13. Hall, *What Christianity Is Not*, 76.
14. Hall, *What Christianity Is Not*, 64.

eras.[15] Searcy describes this truncation of our creedal expression as a form of amnesia motivated by a desire to be seen as relevant and progressive. This narrowing of our doctrinal horizon reflects the arrogance of our time and culture as we judge the faith of our forebears to be deficient, erroneous, or perhaps primitive and underdeveloped. Alas, it is we who are being short-sighted and narrow-minded.

## 5.3 Growing Up and the Quest

A third theme that we have been tracing through this story is the "coming of age" of humanity in the post-1960 Age of Authenticity. On this reading of history, humankind has advanced beyond all the limits of our ancestors. We have outgrown a childish faith that penned us in with all kinds of rules and restrictions in exchange for the promise of keeping us safe in an uncertain and untamable universe. Secular theologians, writing in a time of unprecedented human technological mastery and material prosperity, began to question the ages old distinction between the human and the divine. The language of humans as "co-creators" with God begins to become more prevalent. The dawning sense of human capacity seeks expression in newfound freedoms, notably in the sexual revolution. This climate of the celebration of human freedom is diametrically opposed to the culture of the mainline church of that era. The culture of the church is seen as authoritarian and out of step with the new mood of "expressive individualism" that values freedom of choice and personal autonomy in all areas including the spiritual. This is the beginning of the era of the spiritual quest in which all of the old, pre-packaged answers of traditional religion no longer resonate. The language, the liturgies, the format of church all seem wooden or—in the parlance of the 1960s—"square."

The motif of growing up rests *negatively* on the idea of throwing off tutelage and rejecting structures, norms, and beliefs that unnecessarily constrict human living; and *positively* on the affirmation of human qualities and capabilities. In essence, the motif of growing up is a reaction to life in the immanent frame, particularly as experienced in the Age of Mobilization. It represents a rejection of the conformity and institutionalism of that

---

15. While serving at University Hill Congregation in Vancouver, Searcy encouraged the congregation to maintain a focus on five functions of the church. In addition to Cox's list of *koinonia*, *diakonia*, and *kerygma*, Searcy included *didache* (training in the Way of Christ), and *liturgia* (worship and the sacraments).

CHAPTER 5. FINDING THE HEART OF THE STORY

earlier period. What it inherits from the Age of Mobilization is belief in "progress," the idea that history and human development is moving in a straightforward, linear direction: ever upward! This is where the cultural arrogance of our era enters in—the notion that we have got it all figured out, that we can see what our ancestors could not see. Where their vision was blinkered by religion and tradition, we have emerged into the bright clear sunshine of reason, our view completely unobstructed and without shadow. So John Pentland feels empowered to cast off the limitations of liturgical legislation and denominational bylaws, while Gretta Vosper reminds us that modern science and philosophy leave no room for God to hide anymore.

The positive side of this is the construction of new forms of religious community, forms that are better adapted to the spirituality of the quest in the Age of Authenticity. Pentland envisions a mixed community of radical hospitality, a community that deliberately and consciously seeks to include a large proportion of atheists and agnostics amongst its members. Hillhurst aims to respond to the spirituality of the quest by being an "Age of Spirit" church (in Cox's formulation) inviting participants on a journey that begins with creating a sense of belonging (Bass). Such a community is open to doubt and exploration as participants wrestle with questions of life's meaning. Once again Vosper takes this a step further in her project of creating a fully post-theistic church. Vosper clearly exemplifies the negative and positive aspects of the growing up motif: she seems as strongly motivated by a rejection of the harms of theistic belief as she is by a positive and enthusiastic affirmation of human potential. Her proposal is a clear and uncomplicated offer to those troubled by religion's unbelievability and irrationality, or by its odious restrictions. All those pesky questions about God, the Bible, and Jesus are simply left behind. What remains is a church for grownups.

I think there is a clear trajectory here that connects the secular theologians of the 1960s and their acolytes with proposals like those of Pentland and Vosper. It's not clear to me whether this trajectory was intended or even foreseen by theologians like John A. T. Robinson and Harvey Cox when they penned their best-selling books in the early part of the decade.[16] What is clear is that the notion of growing up was central to their argument. So

16. See Robinson, *Honest to God*, and Cox, *Secular City*. Wendy Fletcher also traces this trajectory as beginning with a (mis)reading of Bonhoeffer's "religionless Christianity" and moving through Robinson, Cox, and on to the work of Diana Butler Bass. See Fletcher, "Bonhoeffer," 14–26.

Berton writes, "Robinson says that twentieth-century man can no longer be treated as a child who needs to believe in charming fairy tales in order to understand eternal truths,"[17] and Cox highlights the images of "growing up, assuming the responsibilities of an heir, executing an accountable stewardship."[18] This language finds a clear echo in Vosper's work and she cites Robinson as an inspiration. The work of Robinson and Cox and popularizers like Berton opened up conversations about the church's core beliefs—about God, Jesus, and the Bible—because the church of that time had lost credibility. The form of religion in the late Age of Mobilization was no longer able to give adequate defense of its beliefs. There are many reasons for this and Taylor provides a great deal of the backstory to this development in the pages of *A Secular Age*, but one way of understanding the story is to say that the church of the Age of Mobilization had overreached in its efforts to manage the whole of society comprehensively. The church as an institution of social control could not survive its collision with the massive social forces unleashed in the postwar era.

But there are (at least) two possible responses here. One way of responding to the problem of the credibility of the church's teaching in an age that lauds scientific truth and distrusts traditional sources of authority is to go back—in the manner suggested by Taylor and Hall above—and engage our doctrines in a conversation that seeks their truth in our current context. Hall's contextual theology reminds us that "gospel is not a fixed message; it is a message that the church itself always has to discover anew, for its aim is to engage, address, and change the actual human situation."[19] The other is to "throw the baby out with the bathwater" and say that since our beliefs have become problematic in our current context we need to leave them behind as we move into the New Age. What we carry forward is a distillation of general principles from which all offending properties are removed. This latter option is made possible by a straight line read of history as progressing in one direction. On this read our current age is the pinnacle of human knowledge and understanding, and we alone in history have the capacity to judge what is true, even when it comes to God. This is the line of thinking that emerges from the growing up thesis. Once we have moved out of a need to be in relationship with all of the problematic parts of our tradition—questions like, How is God possible?, or How could Jesus really be the Son

---

17. Berton, *Comfortable Pew*, 106.
18. Cox, *Secular City*, 130.
19. Hall, *What Christianity Is Not*, 57.

## CHAPTER 5. FINDING THE HEART OF THE STORY

of God?—we are freed to make Christianity mean whatever we want it to mean. Jesus becomes a teacher of ethics, a guru whose disciple we choose to become, for a season perhaps. We are no longer *bound* as baptized persons, constrained to a particular way of living with our neighbor and with God. Or we can go that step further—and it really is only a small step—and set aside God, the Bible, and Jesus altogether, trusting that we have *within us* all that we need to live well in the world.

The stream that connects the secular theology of the 1960s with the proposals of Pentland and Vosper seems like a sensitive and hospitable response to the spirituality of the quest. It takes as its starting place the needs and aspirations of the autonomous and competent individual. It rejects preset answers and unexamined claims to authority. In these ways it is an advance on what came before, but a great deal is lost in the process. It seems as though, for the adherents of this school, all of the furniture of the church—dogma and doctrine, creeds and practices—have become so tainted by the worst aspects of the long centuries of Christendom that they cannot be redeemed, and we are back to this effort to retrieve a distillation of general principles or guiding values. As Hall describes it in this chapter's opening epigraph, we are left with "little more than nostalgia, or a convenient stop-gap to cover the repressed atheism and nihilism of those who 'mourn the death of God' but are afraid to face the death of meaning that accompanies that 'event.'"[20] The models of church that have arisen out of this understanding—including many contemporary United Church congregations and the proposals of Pentland and Vosper—may indeed be open to questers and seekers, inviting doubts and questions and eschewing certainty and dogma, but what they have to offer is a thinned out, watered down residue of the gospel. There is an invitation to go on a journey but the journey seems to lack any sense of destination or particular direction.

Taylor suggests that this is because the journey remains in the immanent frame; it is closed to transcendence. It is only the open window to transcendence that can free us from the malaise we experience bumping up against the walls and bars of our gilded cage. If we truly wish to respond to the spiritual yearnings of questers we need to recover the resources of our whole tradition—what Taylor terms "itineraries" of faith, the paths trod by generations of saints through the two millennia of the church's history. To do this we need to trust that there are ways of upholding and engaging the challenging parts of our tradition that do not rely on the

20. Hall, *What Christianity Is Not*, 152.

methods and approaches of the Age of Mobilization. In others words, we can reject the conformity and authoritarianism that marked how Christianity was presented in that earlier time—and indeed throughout much of the long Christendom era—*without* jettisoning the key elements of the tradition. Taylor suggests that embracing the strangeness—the *in*credibility—of our story actually offers an advantage in our secular age. Seekers today are bombarded by an endless array of self-improvement programs and spiritual or quasi-spiritual avenues that aim to help them live better lives in the immanent frame. But a story that stands in contradistinction to our current cultural norms can rise above the noise: "the very fact that its forms are not absolutely in true with much of the spirit of the age; a spirit in which people can be imprisoned, and feel the need to break out; the fact that faith connects us to so many spiritual avenues across different ages; this can over time draw people towards it."[21] Hall offers a complementary perspective, setting the spirituality of the quest within his discussion of the truth claims of Christianity:

> We turn madly from one false god to another, one ideology to another, one fashionable cause to another, one worldview to another, one alleged truth to another. In our aboriginal restlessness (Augustine), we flee continuously from the One in whom we could find rest—the one Truth that in denying us *securitas* offers us compassion and faithfulness.[22]

We see here again the suggestion that faith can offer what the world cannot: security is a this-worldly goal, something we strive for or try to acquire for ourselves; something that wall-erecting politicians promise to deliver. Faith invites us to exchange security for compassionate embrace. While Hall affirms that this ultimate truth is found in relationship with the transcendent he shares Taylor's appeal to modesty and humility in our claims. He calls for a church that is "oriented toward the Truth" and that is grateful "for all quests for truth and all contributions to the treasury of knowledge that emanate from modest sources that in their own ways and according to their own lights are also oriented toward truth."[23]

---

21. Taylor, *Secular Age*, 533.
22. Hall, *What Christianity Is Not*, 144.
23. Hall, *What Christianity Is Not*, 144–45.

## 5.4 Church and Culture

A final theme that we have been tracing throughout these pages concerns the question of boundaries and the church's relationship to the surrounding culture. Should the church blend in or remain distinct? Should congregations aim to include everyone or are they meant to be enclaves of the especially committed? (This is a recurrence of the phenomenon of "two-speed" spirituality that Taylor sees as the motivation for the various programs of Reform). How do these questions get lived out in the context of pluralism, the world of contested construals which is now our home and will be for the foreseeable future?

One of the key messages of secularists in the 1960s was that the church needed to "get with the world," "listen to the world," to go out into the world. Clergy were encouraged to throw off their collars and to engage with the world unbound from the strictures and baggage of a too "churchy" church. Relevance became a rallying cry, but there is a paradoxical element to this. On the one hand the church of the comfortable pew is faulted for being too embedded in its culture, having imported its norms and hierarchies; yet the same church is seen as being out of touch with key movements and developments in the culture. So Berton questions the absence of "the state of tension which should exist between the Church and society, the divine discontent, which is peculiarly Christian,"[24] suggesting that it is in the nature of the church to be countercultural. Yet, as we have seen repeatedly, Berton and other secularists of the 1960s—as well as Pentland and Vosper—call on the church to divest itself of those elements of its language, practices, and beliefs that put it at odds with contemporary culture. So the church should be *countercultural* in the sense of holding the culture to account, but also *relevant* in the sense of accommodating the culture's language and philosophical and theological preferences. This is explained in part by a past vs. future orientation: the church is seen as being embedded in the culture of the past and irrelevant in the eyes of the emerging culture of the future. This is related to the idea of the linear progress of history which views the past negatively and the future more positively. For the church to "get with the times," then, means that the church ought to align itself with the movement of history in the direction of progress.

The United Church's sense of itself as countercultural emerges from this understanding. Hall writes,

24. Board of Evangelism and Social Service, *Why the Sea*, 2.

> I myself have lived long enough to observe my own denomination, the United Church of Canada, morph from being, certainly, the most culturally established Protestant church in Canada to achieving a countrywide reputation for radicalism and conspicuous divergence from the historical norms and counsels of conventional religion in our country.[25]

This appears to be a fulfillment of what the 1960s critics called for, and indeed a willingness to undertake radical social justice stances has characterized the United Church over the decades. This has been especially apparent in the denomination's affirmation of the eligibility of gay and lesbian persons for ordered ministry in 1988, its advocacy for legal recognition of same-sex marriage in the early 2000s, and its strong commitment to reconciliation with First Nations peoples over the past three decades. Hall notes with caution, however, that this kind of countercultural stance can easily become untethered from its theological roots and become a more conventional secular political stance: "It is no solution of the dangers of establishment when Christians move from an unexamined conventional identification with established power to an easy endorsement of movements of protest against that power."[26] In an era marked by powerful popular movements for civil rights it is all too easy for us to swept up in the world's narratives and to lose the connection to our own. Hall continues,

> We do not have to borrow from others a rationale for environmental stewardship or for concern over marginalized groups or for international economic justice or for world peace. We have an ancient, profound, tried-and-true tradition of ontological and ethical wisdom upon which to draw; and wherever Christian groups have drawn upon that wisdom faithfully and with imagination, they have not only brought an independent voice to the chorus of those who struggle for greater humanity in the earth; they have been welcomed by others because they could contribute insight and perspective often lacking in other protesting groups.[27]

Here Hall is naming the very issues to which Cox and Berton had drawn the church's attention in the 1960s, issues which showed up the church's failings in its function of *diakonia*—economic injustice, racial and ethnic tensions, world peace—as well as issues that have become more crucial in

---

25. Hall, *What Christianity is Not*, 32.
26. Hall, *What Christianity is Not*, 33.
27. Hall, *What Christianity is Not*, 33.

our time, such as the ecological crisis. The challenge for the church is to remain the church even while it participates with others in common efforts. Only then can the church contribute its unique voice and add a perspective otherwise lacking.

The challenge that arises from secular theology's call to make common cause with the world—to take off the collar and drop the distinctive language—is that we risk the church's story being "swallowed up" by the culture's narratives. We have seen that a central element of Pentland's vision for the church is the thinning, or erasure, of the distinctions between church and culture. He wants the church to connect with culture and his proposals suggest ways for the church to reduce the friction, the barriers that get in the way of church reclaiming a place as a popular option in a secular age. For Pentland this involves removing anything that makes the church seem odd, strange, or weird in the eyes of contemporary culture. He is strongly motivated to make the church accessible, understandable, and friendly to this generation. He seems to want to apply every effort to undoing the church's reputation in secular culture—whether it is seen as judgmental and moralizing and dogmatic, or just plain old dull and boring. The truth is that the church has often earned these perceptions because it has behaved in these ways. Pentland understands that the church is not inherently judgmental or inherently boring and to the extent that the church can be presented in ways that challenge these popular conceptions, his is a worthwhile and commendable effort. Taylor's account of the past 500 years reminds us that the church has very often not been at its best, that it has become enmeshed in agendas and programs that are not its own. It is important to critique the church, to call it back to being its best self, to recall it to its roots in the gospel's story of the life, death, and resurrection of Jesus Christ.

However, there is an important question of discernment here, one that takes us back to the baby and the bathwater metaphor. What is essential to the church's story? What makes the church uniquely the church? Pentland seems to suggest that the key element is fostering community, a sense of belonging, a place where people can struggle together with the spiritual questions that arise in our life in a secular world. That certainly sounds like gospel: Jesus was always concerned with community, with crossing boundaries, and with seeking to reduce the friction that separated groups from one another. Pentland is at pains to tell this story in a way that aligns with the values and the needs he perceives in contemporary culture. By making this story understandable and accessible and relevant it may be possible to make the church attractive and popular again. But the church's story affirms that Jesus was more than a community builder, more than a prophet, more than a teacher: the church's story affirms that Jesus was and is the Son of God, that his ministry was the manifestation of God's will for the world, and that the seal and confirmation of all of this was God's resurrection of Jesus from the dead. This is a story that is plainly hard to believe by the lights of contemporary culture. It is not accessible, or understandable, or particularly friendly to the narratives by which we live. But maybe it is not meant to be. Maybe it is meant to be our defense against the ways of the world—the ways of our culture—that are life-destroying, disfiguring, and detrimental to the life God intends for us and the world.

There is general agreement amongst the several positions we have been examining—from the 1960s to our own time—that the story at the heart of the Christian faith is an odd one. On the surface, it fails our time's tests of credibility and relevance. So what does evangelism in our time call us to do? Are we called to the work of translation—making the story accessible, understandable and culture-friendly—which inevitably seems to result in the immanentization—the shrinkage, the scaling back, perhaps the dumbing down—of the story? This seems to be the approach reflected in Pentland's proposal and, once again, Vosper goes further by distilling out timeless values and setting the story as a whole aside, placing it up on the shelf. This approach is predicated on the belief that the only alternative is a modern literalist Fundamentalism which sees Scripture's meaning as fixed and unalterable. This is a fallacy of the modern Western church's division into liberal/progressive and conservative/evangelical/Fundamentalist camps. If we reach back beyond the twentieth century we discover that throughout Christian history there have been multiple ways of reading, interpreting, and attempting to live in response to, Scripture. In other words, it is possible to both stay connected to our strange, old, unbelievable story *and* to seek for what that story has to say to our time and culture. As noted above, it appears as though many have given up on this effort, believing that the key elements of the Christian past cannot be redeemed and must be left behind. We have largely given up on our story, as though we are embarrassed by it or ashamed of it.

In Pentland's case the strangeness of the gospel seems to be sacrificed to the need to excise elements of the tradition that are difficult to understand or accommodate with contemporary culture, and to his efforts to redeem the popularity of the church. For Vosper, who sees religion as inherently divisive, there is no place for any narrative that is rooted in a particular story. In both situations, we give up our particular story in order to accommodate the culture. But giving up on our story leaves us vulnerable to other narratives, as the authors of *Good News In Exile* describe:

> What we first thought of as our humble, self-effacing attempt to articulate the gospel in a "responsible and contemporary way" was a simple demonstration that we had submitted to the powers-that-be. We had given up the battle too soon. In bending over backward to speak to the "modern world," we fell in. In our dialogue with contemporary culture, the traffic moved in one direction. It was always contemporary culture rummaging around in the gospel, telling the gospel what it could and could not believe.[28]

Mark Sayers describes a similar process of evangelism in which the post-Christian secular culture attempts to "colonize" what remains of Christian culture: "with its great mission to prohibit anyone from prohibiting, it seeks to propagate its dogma that there should be no dogma."[29] This is a reading of secularization as a force that seeks to eradicate all particular religious narratives. To some degree both Pentland's and Vosper's approaches reflect this secularist distrust of particularity and the search for universal values that cause no offence. This is perhaps a hangover from the Christendom era, which leaves us continuing to feel obliged to repent of our former hegemonic position, and reticent about making any particular truth claims. The post-Christendom era invites us into a new stance.

Taylor reminds us that in the post-Christendom era, we live in a time of contested narratives, various construals—religious, nonreligious, humanist, and antihumanist, and others—jostling up against one another and fragilizing or undermining each other. In this new context our role is to clearly and cogently present Christian belief—not as the dominant narrative, or necessarily the most popular one. The opportunity in this is that we are freed from the responsibility of shaping a faith perspective that makes sense to everyone or that is universally popular or acceptable. We no longer need to craft a religious narrative to underwrite civilizational order. We live in the era of a spiritual smorgasbord, a belief potluck, and we are called to contribute our best dish—and only that. We don't need to provide the whole meal, or the tables and chairs, or the venue. We just

---

28. Copenhaver, Robinson, and Willimon, *Good News in Exile*, 56.
29. Sayers, *Disappearing Church*, 47.

need to bring our casserole and humbly and joyfully participate in the feast. Hall reminds us that,

> In place of the power-seeking and power-keeping church of the long Christendom centuries, we are returning to the biblical situation of the "little flock," which, *because* it is relatively little and *because* it does not see its destiny as becoming Big, is able in the midst of a highly diverse global situation to be "salt," "yeast," and "light"—concretely, to be a community of peacemaking, of justice seeking, and of stewardship of the good creation.[30]

This vision of a little flock, an outpost or colony of resident aliens,[31] is freed from the need to be popular, relevant, or attractive to the culture which surrounds it. Its purpose is to witness to its fundamentally countercultural story: to proclaim this story in its *kerygma*, to respond to its claims in its *diakonia*, and to model it in its *koinonia*.

We have arrived once more at a paradoxical expression of relevance in many of our United Church congregations today. Like the church of the mid-1960s we are embedded in our culture, having imported its norms, language, and philosophical and theological preferences; yet like that church we are also out of touch with our story and its claims upon us. It is time for us to embrace the opportunities that the end of Christendom provides. Hall records a question asked by the late Catholic theologian Karl Rahner: "Just where is it written that *we* must have the whole 100 per cent?"[32] The post-Christendom visions of church we have been examining seem in some ways to still be bound by the totalizing visions of Christendom-era programs of Reform in that they aim to include everyone. Perhaps it is time to reconsider Reform's attempt at eradication of the gap that separated the highly committed from those who were less willing or able to make such a commitment. Can we in the ruins of mainline Protestantism let go of our need to provide a religious or spiritual home that is acceptable to everyone? Can we be content to just be the casserole and not the full meal? Doing so will perhaps enable us to focus once more on the heart of our story.

---

30. Hall, *What Christianity Is Not*, 39.
31. See Hauerwas and Willimon, *Resident Aliens*.
32. Hall, *What Christianity Is Not*, 116.

## 5.5 Conclusion: Returning to the Heart of the Story

This review and summary has revealed some of the key limitations found in some of the most influential approaches to ecclesiology in the United Church of Canada in the past half century. We have seen how the move away from the particularities of our story—the indispensability of the gospel's witness to the life, death, and resurrection of Jesus Christ—has led to a truncated expression of church. The radically costly call to *agape* and *koinonia* has been domesticated into a vision of a "friendly" church. Twenty centuries of the worldwide church's reflection of the story at the heart of our faith has been distilled into the beautiful, but partial, affirmations found in A New Creed. The revolutions of the 1960s—sexual, intellectual, cultural, and theological—have tempted us to believe that we have outgrown God and that we are the masters of our own destinies. Our desire to be affirmed by contemporary culture—to be popular, to be seen as culturally sophisticated—has led us to adjust our story so that it contains only what secular culture will permit.

This review also suggests the outlines of what might constitute a "course correction" for the denomination, a pathway forward that takes into account the limitations we have noted, as well as Taylor's revision of the secularization thesis and Hall's suggestions for a post-Christendom church. Hall invites us to consider whether a church without Jesus at its heart can long endure and, as we have seen, even suggests that "it is also probable that Christianity would cease to be were its adherents no longer prepared to see anything in Jesus beyond that which could be explained in purely human and rational terms."[33] Clearly the ability to articulate some form of belief in the church's story of the life, death, and resurrection of Jesus Christ is an indispensable characteristic for a robust expression of what it means to be the church. It is this story and the figure of Jesus that is foundational to the church's world-transforming, boundary-shattering *koinonia*. It is this story—and the various articulations of it carried in two millennia of creeds, dogma, and doctrines—with which we must wrestle. It is this particular story—in all its countercultural strangeness—that can stand as a bulwark against some of the worst aspects of the modern, secular, globalized, industrialized, commoditized world in which we live. It is this precious story—like a most treasured family recipe—that is the church's enduring offering to the world God so loves.

33. Hall, *What Christianity Is Not*, 64.

In practical terms, this review suggests steps that individual congregations might take as part of a course correction in order to recover a more catholic and broadly inclusive approach to Christian tradition. A good starting place might be an engagement with the whole of the United Church of Canada's doctrinal tradition, from the Twenty Articles in the Basis of Union right through to the poetic stanzas of A Song of Faith. Such a comprehensive engagement would reveal the ways in which the ancient traditions of the church have been contextualized over time, and perhaps offer fruitful resources for contemporary contemplation of the historic church's witness to the divinity of Jesus. As part of a recent review of the doctrine section of the Basis of Union, the United Church has produced a resource document that would be a suitable starting place for this engagement.[34] Additionally, engaging the doctrines of the church through preaching presents an opportunity for the congregation to reconsider our secularized culture's rejection of doctrine as dry, dusty, and irrelevant. A new resource guide for doctrinal preaching offers examples and methods that help to bridge the gap between contemporary culture and traditional doctrines.[35] The work of Hall could also serve as an excellent resource for congregations attempting to reconcile the best of the United Church's liberal theological heritage with a broader appreciation of the full legacy of the church catholic. Sustained attention to Bible study can help to improve biblical literacy in congregations and prompt renewed engagement with the stories of our tradition. Finally, educational opportunities based on the information presented in these pages could contribute to a reconsideration of secularization and its impact on the church in the post-1960 era, potentially leading to renewed interest in other approaches to ecclesiology.

Having engaged this critical examination of the limits of some of the approaches of the past half century and having begun to suggest the outlines of a renewed commitment to the story at the heart of our faith, we turn now to the constructive work of imagining possible futures for the United Church of Canada.

---

34. United Church of Canada, *Our Words of Faith*.
35. MacLean and Young, *Preaching the Big Questions*.

## Chapter 6. The Next Chapter of the Story

He called the crowd with his disciples, and said to them, "If any want to become my followers, let them deny themselves and take up their cross and follow me. For those who want to save their life will lose it, and those who lose their life for my sake, and for the sake of the gospel, will save it. For what will it profit them to gain the whole world and forfeit their life?

—MARK 8:34–36

United Church minister David Ewart predicts a decade of startling decline for the denomination.[1] Extrapolating trends over the decade 2004–2013, Ewart offers the following estimates of changes by the year 2025: a 31 percent drop in the number of congregations; a 43 percent decline in number of members; a 77 percent decline in weekly worship attendance; a 49 percent drop in financially supporting households; and a 98 percent decline in baptisms. Ewart estimates that professions of faith will reach zero by 2020, and Sunday School membership will hit zero in 2022, the same year that the last wedding will take place, statistically speaking. Clearly the United Church of Canada as an institution is in a state of crisis as a five decade pattern of decline—a decline that began in 1965—shows no signs of abating. The story that I have been telling in these pages does not make a connection between the secularizing tendencies in the United Church of Canada and numerical decline. There are simply too many factors involved to be able to draw that conclusion. Phyllis D. Airhart has suggested that the moves undertaken by the denomination in the 1960s might be seen as adaptive responses that allowed the United Church to survive that tumultuous decade and find a new lease of life, allowing the denomination to carry

---

1. Ewart, "Welcome to the Last Days."

on for five more decades.[2] Whether or not that is the case, the denomination appears to have once more reached a place where its disappearance as an institution is a very real possibility.

The story I have been telling sets aside the question of numbers in order to ask a more fundamental question, a question of faithfulness. What is the church fundamentally? What is non-negotiable for us? What is indispensable for us? As we have seen in our review of secular theology and some more recent proposals for the future of the United Church, over the past five decades we have tended to answer that question in secular terms. We have privileged relevance, connecting to culture, providing community, discerning shared values. Our response to the end of Christendom has tended to look like some version of a survival strategy, desperately holding on, doing all we can, trying anything just to avoid going under. How perverse a choice for a people whose central story is one of death and resurrection!

### 6.1 Two Visions of the Future

In the early 1990s, Marion Best—soon to be elected Moderator of the United Church of Canada—hosted a gathering of lay and order of ministry leaders in the church to consider the denomination's future. The group met for a weekend of conversation and an edited version of their discussions was published under the provocative title *Will Our Church Disappear?* Near the end of the gathering, Best drew the group's attention to the phenomenon of the spiritual quest: "What if someone came to you and said, 'I'm on a spiritual journey. What would I find if I came to your place? What do you have to offer me?'"[3] The first two responses to the question—one given by a lay person and one by an ordained minister—offer a clear illustration of two different visions of what the United Church might be. The first response:

> Friendship. Some sense of community. We have an hour after church just sitting around having coffee. We have a big room open beside the sanctuary and every week the coffee pot is on. And there may be croissants or muffins and so the smells of these warm things coming out of the ovens draw people into the room.[4]

2. Airhart, *Making and Remaking*.
3. Best, *Will Our Church Disappear*, 108.
4. Best, *Will Our Church Disappear*, 108.

## CHAPTER 6. THE NEXT CHAPTER OF THE STORY

The second response:

> Marion, if someone should ask why they should come to our church, I'd have to say it's because we are a community of people who believe that in Jesus we've discovered what it means to be human beings. Or rediscovered it. We are rediscovering it together in one another.... So that's why there's the bread baking and the croissants and the communal life.... We have an old tradition that forms us and challenges us and we form and challenge it. We live in tension with it and we are nourished by it.[5]

Two visions—both of which feature baked goods!—but one with an explicitly theological foundation for its expression of hospitality: coffee, croissants, and community; or coffee, croissants, community, and Jesus. I believe that these two visions are representative of the two main alternative approaches to ministry in the future United Church of Canada. It is to a discussion of these alternatives that I will now turn.

### 6.2 "Secular Church": A Vision of Continuity

Throughout the pages of this book, as we have engaged the story of the United Church of Canada's encounter with secularization—first through the church's response to secular theology in the 1960s and then through our critical examination of the proposals of John Pentland and Gretta Vosper—what emerges quite clearly is the sense that many in our denomination would be more comfortable with "option one" above: coffee, croissants, and community, with perhaps a little bit of Jesus on the side. Vosper attracts a great deal of attention because of the shock value of an avowed atheist in the pulpit of a nominally Christian congregation. But the analysis offered in this book demonstrates that, to a very large degree, Vosper's position is merely a logical next step on a trajectory that connects back to the secular theology of John A. T. Robinson and Harvey Cox. Pentland rejects Vosper's outright atheism as a step too far but I am inclined to read his position in light of Hall's suggestion of "nostalgia, or a convenient stop-gap to cover the repressed atheism and nihilism of those who 'mourn the death of God' but are afraid to face the death of meaning that accompanies that 'event.'"[6] Pentland remains committed to the liberal church project, and to making a

---

5. Best, *Will Our Church Disappear*, 109.
6. Hall, *What Christianity Is Not*, 152.

success of it, but—as he himself acknowledges—the liberal church does not know what to make of Jesus. I must confess a grudging admiration for the intellectual honesty of Vosper's position even as I vehemently disagree with it. At the same I am left with a certain uneasiness over Pentland's project, suspicious that it may—perhaps quite unintentionally—result in nothing more than a stop-gap, resuscitated Christendom church.

I believe that, between them, the proposals of Pentland and Vosper—and the somewhat narrow band of progressive liberal theology they represent—will continue to be very influential in the United Church in the years to come. Their suspicion or outright rejection of transcendence; their dispensing with all of the tricky bits—dogma and doctrine, creeds and practices—and their embrace of generalized distilled truths; their affirmation of the growing up motif and the norms of the Age of Authenticity: in all these ways, these proposals are "in true"[7] with much of the culture of the denomination.

Given the demographics of many United Church congregations, this is perhaps not surprising: the largest group in many congregations is made up of people whose participation stretches back to the 1960s and earlier decades. These are people who are comfortable with the liberal theological tradition and with the secular turn begun in the 1960s. For many, the secular theology of the 1960s was the source of a powerful sense of liberation, setting them free from the shackles of the conventional religious world in which they had been raised. Robinson and Pierre Berton are still spoken of in glowing terms by those who lived through the revolution they unleashed. For this generation, Pentland's proposal holds out the hope of congregational revival—and the return of the young people—for the relatively low cost of manageable and incremental changes, while Vosper has a strong appeal for those among them who see themselves as spiritually advanced grownups, no longer needing the props of childhood religion. An article in the *Observer* chronicled a number of congregations—in addition to Vosper's West Hill United Church—where ministry leaders are experimenting with post-theistic worship and, as we have seen, letters to the magazine indicate high levels of support or sympathy for Vosper's position.[8] We have also seen that Pentland's presentation of the Hillhurst story continues to attract a great deal of attention.

---

7. Taylor, *Secular Age*, 533. Recall Taylor's discussion of the potential advantage of the church's countercultural story, treated in chapter 5 above.

8. Boesveld, "Sacred, Yes. But Is It Church?"

## CHAPTER 6. THE NEXT CHAPTER OF THE STORY

Truth be told, versions of the United Church that look like Hillhurst or West Hill will be powerfully compelling because they are in so many important respects continuous with denominational norms of at least the past half century. These proposals represent evolutionary change—which should reduce levels of resistance—and offer the promise of increased relevance, which adds to their appeal for a generation that continues to value being "with it" and up-to-date. The problem as I see it is that these proposals, for all of their up-to-date appearance, are actually too rooted in the cultural upheavals of the 1960s. Rather than representing a vision of the future, they are pictures of the future drawn by those sympathetic to the liberal cultural revolution that marked that decade: they are *the past's* vision of our future, and we continue to live in their shadow. Vosper describes herself as "a product of the New Curriculum," the Sunday School curriculum that for the first time widely disseminated the fruits of liberal theology when it was introduced in 1964.[9] Pentland grew up in the same era. It is as if the battles of the 1960s—the fight against rigid, authoritarian, and downright *dull* expressions of Christian faith—keep being fought, long after the so-called enemies have been vanquished. The United Church of today is not dogmatic or doctrinal; hardly anyone is asked to recite the Apostles Creed; other-worldly, salvationist, afterlife theology is largely absent from our pulpits and Bible studies; many social conservatives and evangelicals have left—either over issues like the New Curriculum in the 1960s, or over the decision to allow the ordination of lesbian and gay persons in the 1980s. The denomination has embraced the ministry of the laity, and the old clerical caste which seemed to control the denomination has been thoroughly routed.

Yet many in our denomination continue to construct models of the future that are predicated on solving the perceived problems of the past. Not long ago, I attended a Presbytery consultation in another part of the Conference in which I serve. At that gathering, clergy and lay leaders from small town and rural congregations offered reflections on what they were experiencing in this ongoing time of transition in the church. Some spoke of their buildings and properties as assets, not necessarily for ministry but for community service; they envisioned informal networks of church and community groups. Others defined their ministry as social justice and assistance to children and seniors. A minister recounted an experiment with fellowship in a restaurant, gathering people for meaningful conversations,

---

9. United Church Observer Staff, "Beyond Belief."

describing it as "church in a format they could actually tolerate." Someone else described replacing a church building with a newly built structure resembling a community hall so as not to offend anyone uncomfortable with the idea of church. Such comments are generally well-intentioned and they do reflect common cultural stereotypes of the church in our secular age. But it is a mark of how secularized the church has become when those inside the church accept the culture's perceptions uncritically. It is as if some kind of "internalized ecclesiophobia" is operative in the liberal mainline.

Two observations struck me at the time: first, the belief that the church's greatest assets are its buildings and properties and not the gospel and Jesus; and second, the amount of contempt that many church people—especially church leaders—have for the church. If we inside the church feel this way about it—as though we are embarrassed about our story and ashamed of our history—is it any wonder that our evangelism is failing? In that gathering I also observed how leaders seemed unwilling to accept responsibility for the ways we have been failing to be the church. Rather than connecting our own negative views of the church and our embarrassment over the odd story of Jesus to the diminishment and aging of our congregations, we continue to seek ways of being relevant to the culture and useful to the world, deploying our assets in that project. Yet, as Stanley Hauerwas and William H. Willimon remind us, "an accommodationist church, so intent on running errands for the world, is giving the world less and less in which to disbelieve,"[10] opening the door to a post-theistic version of church.

I suspect that this secularized vision of our denomination is so entrenched that it will continue to be a common or normative presentation of the United Church for the foreseeable future. Another of the conversations recorded in *Will Our Church Disappear?* concerns United Church identity. One participant offered this summary:

> I think our identity as a church is in our openness and inclusiveness.... People in our community, if they want something broader than the narrowness of some denominations, tend to approach the United Church.... But maybe (and I have a lot of fear about this) we need to be losing our identity. Maybe part of the call is to work with people of goodwill in other faith communities, or wherever there are people working for justice and compassion.... That

---

10. Hauerwas and Willimon, *Resident Aliens*, 94.

## CHAPTER 6. THE NEXT CHAPTER OF THE STORY

makes us, as a church, less visible. We can no longer simply say, "This is the United Church of Canada at work!"[11]

This is a more recent example of what Airhart describes as the willingness in the 1960s to "risk theological anonymity and denominational invisibility" as the church moved out into the community in service.[12] As we have seen in some of the reflections in the Presbytery consultation above, this remains an enduring and compelling call for many in our denomination. Another participant in the *Will Our Church Disappear?* discussion described the United Church's willingness to offer rites of passage to those who are not otherwise connected to a faith community: "That scares some people because they feel we haven't got any guidelines. We'll marry anybody, bury anybody. But I think we're being challenged to let go some of our denominational identity so that we can minister to that necessity."[13] What these comments suggest to me is a possible role for the United Church of the future as "a church for a secular age," or "a church for people who don't like church," or perhaps simply, a "secular church." This vision would be consistent with much of the current mood in many United Church congregations. A possible model here may be the Sunday Assembly movement in the United Kingdom cited in chapter 5, with its mantra of "live better, help often, wonder more."

Our world could no doubt use more places of genuine hospitality, places that draw people in with the fragrance of friendship. The world could no doubt benefit from more people wanting to live better and to be compassionate and open to wonder. While I suspect that the animating spirit of this vision is rooted more in secular humanism than in the gospel, efforts aimed at providing compassionate service in a hurting world are not to be derided. The question is not, Are they doing any good? or Are such projects worthwhile? For our purposes, the question is, Are they church? Clearly some people in the United Church would be comfortable transitioning to some kind of post-theistic, post-Christian, post-church enterprise.

---

11. Best, *Will Our Church Disappear*, 48–49.
12. Airhart, *Church with the Soul of a Nation*, 299.
13. Best, *Will Our Church Disappear*, 49.

## 6.3 A Divided Church?

A few years ago, the *United Church Observer* published a record of a conversation/debate between Vosper—described as an atheist—and another United Church minister, Connie denBok—described as a believer.[14] In response to a question about the capacity or flexibility of the denomination "to employ all sorts of minsters, even those who no longer accept what the church professes to believe," denBok offers her assessment of the church:

> We are, in my opinion, a kind of anarchistic loose alliance of individuals and congregations, held together by a common property owner, by a common love for nobody telling us exactly what we should do. We have *that* in common. . . . Ours is a branch of the church family that seems to have lost its purpose and sense of direction. Our family tree looks like it will become extinct unless we find a way to connect with God and the Christian scriptures.

Vosper concurs:

> One of the things the United Church failed to do, as many other mainline denominations failed to do as they moved away from a salvationist theology, was to name why we come together. We got close to having those important conversations in the 1960s, but we veered away because we were afraid it was going to tear the fabric apart, and we didn't want to deal with that.

As the conversation continues, Vosper offers her definition of the work of the church:

> VOSPER: Living in right relationship with others, with the planet—that is what I have seen and distilled as the essence of the work of The United Church of Canada.
>
> DENBOK: Of course. But you don't need church for any of that. The only thing church has to offer that other organizations don't do better is the God thing.[15]

Vosper makes a plea for a post-theistic future for the denomination as a whole before conceding that it is now too late:

> VOSPER: We're two, three generations too late. We should have kept with this work in the 1960s.

14. United Church Observer Staff, "Beyond Belief."
15. In the terminology of Jim Collins's *Good to Great*, God—or Jesus—is the church's "hedgehog concept." See Collins, *Good to Great*

## CHAPTER 6. THE NEXT CHAPTER OF THE STORY

DENBOK: Or honourably split, way back when.

VOSPER: Honourably split, way back when. Exactly.

The conversation concludes with a recognition that the United Church as it currently exists is "like some dysfunctional extended family; you can't divorce family members." The history of Protestantism, of course, suggests otherwise and this conversation reveals the particular United Church of Canada version of a phenomenon emerging *within* many branches of Christianity today: a growing fault line between the progressive and orthodox wings of each denominational family. DenBok notes that the United Church of Canada "seems to have lost its purpose and sense of direction" and suggests a path to renewal that embraces some return to more orthodox belief: "our family tree looks like it will become extinct unless we find a way to connect with God and the Christian scriptures." Vosper concurs that a shared sense of purpose has been lost, due to a failure of nerve in the 1960s which otherwise might have led the denomination to pursue a post-theistic vision at that early date—and she remains committed to pursuing a progressive vision for the denomination that is focused on "living in right relationship with others, with the planet." The women both acknowledge the lack of a shared vision for the future of the United Church and then argue for two very different futures. Given that there are a myriad of other positions in the denomination—leaders and congregations who do not see themselves in either the vision of Vosper or that of denBok—this suggests that any future vision for the denomination will be contested.

What keeps the conversation about divorce at bay for now is the reality that the progressive side of the conversation is clearly the dominant voice in the denomination as a whole. Those in the orthodox camp are a minority, although the denominational conversation about Vosper's provocative position may be contributing to increased delineation of positions. As noted in chapter 4, there is a process currently underway to determine the ongoing effectiveness of Vosper for ministry in the United Church, a process that may result in her being barred from service in the denomination. Should the review determine that her atheism is an impediment to her continuing to serve in ministry, it is difficult to speculate what the wider impact of such a ruling might be. There are clearly a number of clergy leaders in the United Church who hold similar views to Vosper, and a wider circle of leaders and church members who are supportive of her continued service and who will be deeply concerned over her expulsion. Such an outcome may test the limits of this extended, dysfunctional family to hold together.

### 6.3.1 Postscript—September 2016: Review Findings

The committee reviewing Vosper's effectiveness for ministry in the United Church of Canada issued its report on September 7, 2016. The committee found, by a 19 to 4 majority, "that Rev. Gretta Vosper is not suitable to continue serving in ordered ministry in The United Church of Canada."[16] Basing its decision on the four statements of United Church doctrine described in chapter 5, the majority report noted that "what Ms. Vosper believes and practices today is very different from the doctrine of The United Church of Canada. Ms. Vosper has stripped worship, prayer, baptism and communion at West Hill of their continuity with the Church, their connection with scripture, and the presence of God."[17] The committee has recommended that a hearing be conducted by the national office of the church to consider whether Vosper will be placed on the denomination's "Discontinued Service List (Disciplinary)," removing her from ministry. There will be further hearings in this process before any final decisions are made in regards to Vosper's eligibility to continue serving in ministry, meaning that the process is still far from over.

At this point, what is clear is that the United Church has been pressed by circumstances to define more clearly the limits of its beliefs. The majority report notes that "although The United of Canada is a big tent, welcoming a diversity of theological beliefs, Ms. Vosper is so far from centre of what holds us together as a **united** church that we have concluded that she is not suitable to continue as an ordained minister in our Church."[18] This outcome is largely due to Vosper's challenge to the church to clarify its beliefs. Given the breadth of territory covered by the United Church's four articulations of doctrine over the past century, a case can be made that Vosper could have found a place for herself somewhere within the big tent, had she wanted to. As we have seen in the discussion of Vosper's position in these pages,

---

16. Toronto Conference Interview Committee, "Report of Conference Interview Committee," 31.

17. Toronto Conference Interview Committee, "Report of Conference Interview Committee," 35.

18. Toronto Conference Interview Committee, "Report of Conference Interview Committee," 36.

however, her sense of integrity does not allow for any fudging of her beliefs. She does not want to be in the same tent as people who hold theistic beliefs, because of what she perceives as the inherent divisiveness and violence of such belief. Because of her strong commitment to that position, Vosper has forced the denomination's hand. I suspect that the repercussions from this decision will be strong and long-lasting. This could signal another ending for the United Church of Canada. At the very least what seems to be ending is the denomination's capacity to maintain a certain theological nebulousness, a looseness of definition that allowed for different interpretations so long as nobody pressed the issue too closely. Vosper's unwillingness to play the game of multiple meanings, nudges and winks, and fingers-crossed-behind-the-back affirmations of doctrine has likely spelled the beginning of the end of this almost century-long method of accommodation of difference in the denomination. As the argument of this book no doubt suggests, I am not an advocate for theological nebulousness, but I recognize the importance of this orientation for the United Church of Canada. Looseness of definition has allowed a wide variety of believers, questers, doubters, and questioners to find a home in the United Church. Theological looseness has been an important plank in the structure of the denomination. Can the denomination long endure once this plank is removed? Only time will tell how this will play out, but the outcome of this process further adds to the burdens the United Church will face in the coming years.

### 6.4 "Progressive Orthodoxy": A Vision of Renewal

In a further excerpt from the conversation with Vosper cited above, den-Bok offers a vision of a renewed United Church of Canada—one that is rooted in its story and its tradition and yet responsive to the contemporary spiritual quest:

> In spite of the story-line that we have outgrown God and religious practice, I'm finding a generation hungry for God and for a spirituality that engages them in an encounter with the Other. The God story is very much focused on somebody who is not me, who is in relationship with me; someone whom I cannot remake according to my particular tastes; someone who has thoughts and opinions that are different from my own.[19]

---

19. United Church Observer Staff, "Beyond Belief."

She is certainly not alone in her presentation of a more orthodox version of Christian faith, and in the discussion she describes the formation of informal clusters in the church, spaces that draw together like-minded clergy in our diverse denomination. Over the past few years, I have been introduced to such groups, including a recently formed Facebook group for United Church clergy "who long for a Christ-centred, discipleship-oriented approach to church and ministry, but aren't finding it in the wider church." There appears to be growing interest in such an approach, especially amongst younger clergy and those recently entering into ministry.[20] In what follows I will sketch my own personal vision of what such an approach might entail. Whether this sort of approach will prove attractive for many congregations in the United Church of Canada, I cannot say; what I am attempting to do is describe a vision of what the United Church could be if it both held on to its valuable and distinctive contributions to the wider Christian tradition, and took account of the Taylorian critique of its recent history described in these pages.

As a tentative description for such a vision for the church, I suggest the term "progressive orthodoxy." The first word in the term, *progressive*, indicates embrace of the denomination's heritage of support for social justice, right relationships, and efforts at engagement with those at the margins. The second word in the pair, *orthodoxy*, asserts that, in the church, progressive values are given their shape and meaning and purpose by the gospel. Progressives who cannot abide the parameters set by the story of the life, death, and resurrection of Jesus Christ may choose to be part of the "secular church" described above, a Sunday Assembly congregation, or a secular humanist organization. Orthodox believers who are uncomfortable with elements of the liberal theological heritage—or whose understanding of Scripture does not admit of the full acceptance of the ministry of LGBTQ persons, for example—have many options for Christian fellowship in a wide variety of denominations. Combining these two elements into *progressive orthodoxy* holds the promise of celebrating the fruit of the United Church of Canada's particular charisms as one branch of the Christian family, while the branch remains firmly affixed to the larger tree of Christianity rooted in the story revealed in Scripture.

---

20. A recent *Observer* article offers some confirmation of this. See Pieta Wooley, "Young, Smart and Into Jesus," *United Church Observer*, September 2016, accessed September 8, 2016, http://ucobserver.org/faith/2016/09/millennial_ministers/.

## CHAPTER 6. THE NEXT CHAPTER OF THE STORY

What might such a vision for the church include? It is beyond the scope of this work to draw up a comprehensive model for a progressive orthodox expression of the United Church of Canada; perhaps this could be a suitable field of enquiry for future study. What follows is an attempt to outline a number of crucial foundational elements that would enable a recovery of a more orthodox theological position within the context of a progressive denominational tradition. These elements include: the centrality of Jesus; a willingness to embrace the post-Christendom humiliation of the church;[21] a willingness to assume a countercultural stance; and a willingness to engage the adventure of "being the church."

Douglas John Hall reminds us of what must be foundational to a vision of a renewed church. In the Dedication of *What Christianity Is Not*, Hall addresses his grandchildren, offering them the wisdom gleaned from a lifetime's contemplation of the mystery at the center of reality: "Christianity professes and confesses that at the center of this universal mystery there is ... *love*. Eternal, forgiving, expectant, suffering love." Hall continues:

> That is why the life, death, and resurrection of Jesus, called the Christ, is the central image and narrative of the Christian faith: because his story announces so poignantly and unforgettably how love, despite all that negates and demeans it, is the origin and end of all that is: the *alpha* and *omega*, as the Scriptures say.[22]

Hall suggests that there can be no church without a recognition of the divinity of Jesus. Not a blind affirmation, and not anything close to a full understanding of the mystery of Jesus as God's Son, the second person of the Trinity, fully human and fully divine. But a progressive orthodox stance means that we must be willing to offer more than an affirmation of his goodness, or of his morality, or of his wisdom, or of the value and utility of his teachings. We must be willing to stand under this story, to wrestle with the patterns of obedience it suggests to us. We cannot remove the divinity of Jesus from the story and still have a coherent story. We cannot distill out general principles common to all religions, write the particularity of Jesus out of the story, and still call it Christianity. Doing so leaves us with some version of the first option discussed above: a society of good-hearted, well-intentioned, hospitable humanists. A progressive orthodoxy requires us to engage critically and prayerfully with the story at the heart of our faith.

---

21. Hall uses the term "humiliation" to describe the post-Christendom status of the church.

22. Hall, *What Christianity Is Not*, xv.

In the context of the post-Christendom humiliation of the church, Hall urges us to eschew dreams of the power, privilege, and numerical strength that were hallmarks of the Christendom church and to rekindle our kinship with the crucified one. Power, privilege, and cultural relevance can too easily blind us to what our mission is, lulling us into the comfortable illusion that the church is a destination in itself. Hall reminds us of the *apostolic* mission of the church, that we are a people commissioned, sent out into the world. Describing God's habit of electing the small and powerless, Hall writes:

> For Jerusalem, on the contrary, the few exist for the sake of the ... many. The elect are not a golden minority who have risen above "the herd" (Nietzsche!); they are not a select coterie who live on another, higher plane of being. Rather, for the tradition of Jerusalem the few are (yes!) *chosen*—but chosen for a purpose infinitely more generous and expansive than their own being and destiny. They are chosen as witnesses to a new reality intended for all.[23]

It is our smallness and vulnerability that allows us to right-size our relationship with God and our relationships with others.

The modern age has encouraged us to think of ourselves as powerful, as grownups who have come of age and are ready to be co-creators with God, masters of the universe even. Remembering whose we are, and the story of which we are a part, we discover how small our imaginations are, how puny our scope of concern, how limited our compassion. We realize that we have become preoccupied with the maintenance of the institutional church and the cultivation of our assets, forgetting that none of it actually belongs to us and that instead it has been entrusted to us for the sake of God's mission in the world. Our arrogance is even apparent in our decisions to close churches and distribute assets in the community, as we often mistake our own agendas for God's priorities.

The shift that is called for here is a move away from regarding the church as a human services organization providing programs to an understanding of the church as a community rooted in the gospel. A progressive orthodox church is a humble and vulnerable church, cognizant of its dependence upon God for its daily bread and unencumbered by the maintenance of a myriad of services and programs only tangentially related to the gospel. It will seek to stay rooted in its story and continually discern the mission to which it is being called by God.

23. Hall, *What Christianity Is Not*, 102–3.

## CHAPTER 6. THE NEXT CHAPTER OF THE STORY

Hall ponders what this might mean for the mainline church still rich in assets: "Does it mean getting rid of church properties that are no longer used to capacity? Perhaps, in some cases. Perhaps not, in others."[24] The key will be a renewed focus on being the church rather than on maintaining an institution and its services. As noted above in the discussion of the presbytery consultation, we have in many instances become confused about what the church's assets are and what our purpose is. Being the church ultimately does not require buildings or paid staff. Conversely, were we to focus on being the church and getting clear on our purpose, we might find a great deal of interest and support for such a vision of renewed congregational life.

Hauerwas and Willimon also invite us to comprehensively turn away from the Constantinian legacy of the church as underwriter of civilizational order and cultural guardian:

> From a Christian point of view, the world needs the church, not to help the world run more smoothly or to make the world a better and safer place for Christians to live. Rather, the world needs the church because, without the church, the world does not know who it is. The only way for the world to know that it is being redeemed is for the church to point to the Redeemer by being a redeemed people. The way for the world to know that it needs redeeming, that it is broken and fallen, is for the church to enable the world to strike hard against something which is an alternative to what the world offers.[25]

This is a vision of the church as countercultural. Not because culture is inherently bad, but because it is not *true*: it does not offer the truth about reality, but instead purveys a whole host of alluring illusions. This is not a call for a complete withdrawal from culture. Instead, it is a call for reorientation and rebalancing of the relationship between the church and culture. Mark Sayers cites the work of historian Arnold Toynbee in a discussion of "creative minorities" and a pattern of withdraw/return in which minorities retreat from the sometimes misleading or disorienting narratives of culture into the presence of God, before engaging the culture with healing truth.[26] The church no longer "runs errands" for the culture, or serves as its "conscience," offering cover for a variety of political agendas, or seeks to make itself appealing to the culture, even at the cost of its own integrity.

---

24. Hall, *What Christianity Is Not*, 121.
25. Hauerwas and Willimon, *Resident Aliens*, 94.
26. Sayers, *Disappearing Church*, 49–51.

This is a vision of a church with backbone, a church that has recovered a sense of integrity as to its identity and its story. This is a church that does not need to be popular, but only seeks to be faithful—not only for its own sake but for the sake of the culture and the world God loves. A progressive orthodox church will respectfully engage with culture while maintaining its self-respect. It will not allow itself to be distracted or its mission to be distorted by the culture's judgments or demands.

Hauerwas and Willimon remind us that the primary role of the church is to "be the church" as they reflect on the Sermon on the Mount:

> The sermon implies that it is as isolated individuals that we lack the ethical and theological resources to be faithful disciples. The Christian ethical question is not the conventional Enlightenment question, How in the world can ordinary people like us live a heroic life like that? The question is, What sort of community would be required to support an ethic of nonviolence, marital fidelity, forgiveness, and hope such as the one sketched by Jesus in the Sermon on the Mount?[27]

This is a beautiful, powerful, and compelling vision of the church as *koinonia*. This question is comprehensive enough to serve as a foundation for the mission of any congregation. What kind of community would we need to be to support those who gather here to keep their promises, live in right relationship, contribute to healing, mend what is broken? What would it take for us to become a community in which we genuinely serve one another, sharing one another's joys and burdens? How much deeper and richer is this vision than that of the church of the comfortable pew, in which everyone shows up looking their Sunday best, and if things are going poorly they prefer to stay home rather than be seen "looking like this"?

This vision also transcends the liberal church paradigm of "friendliness" that remains on the level of mutual interests but keeps real life at arm's length. It pushes past the notion of church as provider of spiritual services that mostly offers affirmation of God's love without the challenge of God's call. A progressive orthodox church invites its members not just to Sunday fellowship, but to share life, "to join up, to become part of a movement, a people,"[28] recognizing that

> the most creative social strategy we have to offer is the church. Here we show the world a manner of life the world can never

---

27. Hauerwas and Willimon, *Resident Aliens*, 80.
28. Hauerwas and Willimon, *Resident Aliens*, 21.

## CHAPTER 6. THE NEXT CHAPTER OF THE STORY

> achieve through social coercion or governmental action. We serve the world by showing it something that it is not, namely, a place where God is forming a family out of strangers.[29]

Here *koinonia* becomes *diakonia*, not as a new outreach program of the church, but as a result of the church being the church.

This brief description of some of the core elements that would support the recovery of a more orthodox position within the progressive tradition of the United Church raises some significant questions. Whereas the vision of a "secular church" described above is clearly in continuity with many of the shifts that have occurred in the United Church since the 1960s, the vision of a progressive orthodox church described here is clearly discontinuous with much that has occurred in the denomination over the last half century. It explicitly rejects some of the "lessons" of secularization in light of Taylor's undermining of the standard secularization thesis, its subtraction stories, and its linear read of historical progress. Is this still recognizably the United Church of Canada? Would such an *orthodox* vision of the church still respect the denomination's strong *progressive* heritage—such as welcoming the ministry of LGBTQ persons, pursuing right relationship with First Nations peoples, and advocating care for creation? Would congregations in this mold still leave room for doubts and questions and differences, or does this represent a return to a more authoritarian, traditional past? I turn now to a discussion of the practical implications of such a vision for United Church congregations.

## 6.5 Getting from Here to There

Without a doubt, this vision of progressive orthodoxy would not be easy to implement in many United Church congregations. The vast majority of congregations in the presbytery in which I serve are simply too far away from this vision for it to be a compelling or attractive option. Additionally, this vision requires a strong commitment to discipleship and a willingness to push beyond the "friendliness" and the charitable outreach that characterize many liberal mainline congregations. Eddie Gibbs sets out the daunting mission before us, noting that mainline denominations

> struggle with the challenge of trying to turn around consumerist churches consisting of undiscipled church members. The apostles

---

29. Hauerwas and Willimon, *Resident Aliens*, 83.

first discipled a group of people until they became a church. We face the opposite problem of turning church members into disciples, which is to put the cart before the horse.[30]

This challenge suggests that renewal may require new congregations, either through church plants or through attracting a significant number of new participants into an established congregation. In this latter situation, a two-track strategy—continuing to provide resources and support to the legacy congregation while investing in developing a renewed congregation—could help to ease anxiety through a transition period.

This vision of renewal, while somewhat discontinuous with recent developments in the United Church of Canada, represents a retrieval of the broader tradition that characterized the denomination before the 1960s. As we have seen, the official doctrine of the United Church still affirms the ancient creeds of the church and the evangelical doctrines of the Reformation, as well as the insights of neo-orthodoxy, alongside its liberal theological heritage. A progressive orthodox United Church is one that would seek to push beyond the limitations of a reliance upon only one creedal statement, the 1968 New Creed, to recover the challenges and adventure of a broader engagement with the doctrines of the universal church.

Now-retired United Church minister Edwin Searcy, while serving the University Hill congregation in Vancouver, pioneered a model of a United Church congregation that sought to recover a deeper rootedness in the traditions of the church. Searcy employed a model of the marks of the ancient church, including the three embraced by Cox in *The Secular City*—*kerygma*, *diakonia*, and *koinonia*—but with the addition of two further functions—*liturgia* (worship and the sacraments) and *didache* (training in the Way of Jesus). The retrieval of *liturgia* and *didache* essentially fill in the gaps that we have seen in the secularized liberal mainline. Pentland and Vosper seek to radically reinterpret or dispense with the sacraments and elements of traditional worship practice because they have lost their meaning, and their proposals take a negative view of dogma and doctrine as essentially irredeemable. The recovery of *liturgia* and *didache* is a countermove that enables the congregation to take a second look at the gifts of our heritage. The University Hill congregation now describes itself as "evangelical, catholic, Biblically-centred, and liberal and inclusive."[31] These

30. Gibbs, *Rebirth of the Church*, 67.

31. University Hill Congregation Ministry Profile and Search Committee, "Ministry Profile and Search Report," 2.

## CHAPTER 6. THE NEXT CHAPTER OF THE STORY

are a fitting set of hallmarks for a vision of a renewed, progressive orthodox, United Church ecclesiology.

As suggested by University Hill's description of itself as liberal and inclusive, a recovery of a more orthodox orientation and a renewed commitment to discipleship need not conflict with the United Church's heritage of commitment to social justice action; in many instances, it would strengthen this commitment. What would change are the underlying justifications for such action: rather than being grounded in liberal ideology or the generic values of humanism, such action would be an expression of our baptismal commitment to the way of Jesus. As Peter Berger reminded us—and many others have testified—"What would *really* be revolutionary would be to take seriously the beliefs of the New Testament, of the early Christian confessions, or of the sixteenth-century Reformers."[32] A church that encouraged disciples to take the gospel—along with doctrine and dogma—seriously would foster a radically transformative *koinonia* and *diakonia* that would extend and deepen this traditional charism of the denomination. And as Hall insists, "we do not have to borrow from others a rationale for environmental stewardship or for concern over marginalized groups or for international economic justice or for world peace."[33] These causes are a natural expression of our discipleship. Setting them in the context of our discipleship rather than say, our citizenship, should serve to strengthen our commitment, making it less of an option and more of a commandment.

As to the concern about whether a more orthodox turn indicates a return to the rigidity and authoritarianism of the past, University Hill's understanding of itself as liberal, inclusive, and catholic is an affirmation of its broad and critical orientation to tradition and of its openness to doubt and questioning as components of the life of faith. To a large degree this is a matter of what problem one is trying to solve. Within the contemporary United Church of Canada, permission to doubt and to question is not generally the problem: we have that in spades! What we have far less of is permission to believe. A progressive orthodoxy celebrates and cherishes our story as a gift and treasure, without allowing it to be turned into a weapon or a tool of dehumanization. With humility we engage the whole of our tradition and invite others to contribute their readings; we accept the provisionality of our interpretations without succumbing to relativism.

---

32. Berger, "Relevance Bit Comes to Canada," in Kilbourn, *Restless Church*, 75.
33. Hall, *What Christianity Is Not*, 33.

Having established that a progressive orthodox vision is consistent with the historical traditions of the United Church, and having suggested some of the key elements of such a vision, I turn now to a brief sketch of what some of this might look like in practice with reference to the five marks of the church practiced at University Hill Congregation: *kerygma*, *diakonia*, *liturgia*, *didache*, and *koinonia*.

*Kerygma*. To suggest that the story of the life, death, and resurrection of Jesus must be at the center of the church's life means that there must be a commitment to biblical, gospel-centered preaching. Too often in the liberal mainline church, preaching perversely avoids the good news and seeks to offer good advice instead. Too often, Scripture functions like a soup bone that adds a little flavor to an otherwise informative lecture on politics, economics, sociology, or psychology. Too often, sermons seek to explain or demystify the gospel and make it safe for spiritual consumers who are looking for a few tips on how to be slightly better behaved in the coming week. Sermons need to proclaim the good news in all its surprising and disruptive power. God loves us as we are, yes; but God does not want to leave us as we are. Jesus has bigger plans for us than tweaking our manners just a little bit. Church needs to be less like a trip to the spiritual spa and more like an existential encounter.

*Diakonia*. Embracing the opportunities provided by the humiliation of the church means embracing our smallness, vulnerability, and dependence. It means relinquishing our focus on institutional survival and "keeping the lights on" and turning instead to a focus on the mission to which we are called. This is not to say that "the building" is the problem; too often the problem is a lack of gospel-fired imagination. We prioritize looking after ourselves, convincing ourselves that maintenance of the building is an essential ingredient for our ability to do mission, but all too often we do not get to the mission and our focus remains on providing services to members. At other times, we set building and mission in opposition to one another and make the decision to sell the building and distribute the proceeds. This also reflects a lack of vision and a lack of attention to God's mission. If we stop engaging Scripture seriously and look instead to the general principles of good citizenship, we end up making decisions formed by the norms of middle class participation in liberal democracy and not by the commands of the gospel. *Diakonia* invites us to discern how we might share what we have with others not as a service-providing institution, but as a neighbor. It requires a commitment

## CHAPTER 6. THE NEXT CHAPTER OF THE STORY

to getting to know our neighbors, forming relationships, and sharing our life. We can do this no matter how much or how little we have to share. Having little to share is perhaps preferable as it keeps us out of the Christendom church's habits of arm's length charity.

*Liturgia* and *Didache*. These two elements were missing from Cox's list of the functions of the church, and the visions of church that emerge from secular theology's influence seem to have little time for these elements. It is as though they represent a kind of foreign language whose meaning has been lost. When the sacraments lose their meaning, when they become unmoored from the story of what our Triune God has done and is doing in our world, they become empty rituals, dry and uninteresting. Our lack of attention to the sacraments in the United Church has left clergy and congregation members with a sense that we are going through the motions without knowing why. Our teaching ministry—*didache*—has also atrophied as we are no longer able to say what we believe and have become embarrassed by the language of our ancestral creeds and doctrines. Our seeking after relevance leads us to jettison these parts of our communal life that seem most arcane in the eyes of our culture. Having lost our own connection to their life giving power, they seem small things to give up. We need to restore both our sacramental life and our engagement with the creeds and doctrines of the church. This requires a commitment to sustained teaching in the congregation through workshops, preaching, and practice in the context of worship. As an initial step it may require denominational support for clergy leaders to become (re)acquainted with the practices and teachings of the church. Such efforts will enable us to move from a sense of embarrassment over these countercultural elements of our communal life, and to instead view them as gifts, mysteries even, that we can share with those on the spiritual quest.

*Koinonia*. I believe this is the crucial gift of the church. It is certainly key to any renewal of congregational life. A commitment to *koinonia* means that we dare to push beyond the country club or seniors club rules of engagement for church, and instead commit to sharing life together. It means moving from donating to the congregation's food bank to ensuring that the person sitting next to you in the pew is not going hungry. This is more than community; it is more than family: it is to become family as Jesus redefines family in the gospels. We are often told that people today lack places of community and belonging, and many congregations aspire to provide a sense of family or community. We need to do more than that as church. This will also require teaching and preaching that invites engagement with the gospel and reminds the congregation of the comprehensiveness of their commitment to one another. This could perhaps be enhanced through the use of small groups or other approaches that invite increased commitment and accountability.

What I have suggested here hardly constitutes an action plan or a how-to guide for congregations seeking to move to a progressive orthodoxy orientation. This is partly due to the fact that, as noted above, such an effort falls outside the bounds of this book and partly due to the fact that each congregation has its own context. The main reason for the roughness of my sketch, however, is my conviction that such a plan or a guide represents a second order concern: plans and programs and strategies are all secondary to the question of core beliefs. What each congregation needs to wrestle with is what it believes, in particular what it believes about Jesus. Once there is some clarity about that, the rest of it is not rocket science. How could it be? The way to be the church was invented by people who had neither rockets nor modern science, nor any of our techniques and technologies that we apply to the problems of the church. Without clarity as to what we believe about Jesus, all the technologies and techniques we apply can grow our churches, at least for a time, but to what end?

## 6.6 Conclusion

The vision being sketched here—what I have termed progressive orthodoxy—is a vision of a church that refuses to believe that its survival in a secular age must come at the cost of throwing its treasure overboard. The church's treasure—the gospel—is indispensable: without it we are no longer the church. Jettisoning the gospel may allow us to survive as an institution, but only as a zombie institution continuing to live off of the diminishing returns of the investments of the saints who came before us. The gospel is not an embarrassment, something we should be ashamed of—it is our life, and Christians, and the Church, have no life without it. The gospel is always inherently relevant; it always has something to say to every time, place, and culture. As Hall reminds us, we sometimes have to work at it but what we ought not to do is give up the effort, put it up on the shelf in frustration, and make up some new religion: a golden calf to stand in place of the God witnessed to in Scripture.

## CHAPTER 6. THE NEXT CHAPTER OF THE STORY

A progressive orthodox church seeks to hold on to the gifts of our tradition—the wisdom of the saints, the witness of the martyrs—and it seeks to follow the paths they have trod. Such a church rejects the belief that our wisdom exceeds that of all those who have gone before. Instead, this church humbly seeks to attach itself to the company of those who have responded to the paradoxical call to save their lives by being willing to lose them. Our participation in the deep wisdom of this tradition and its practices is our offering to a world of seekers tossed to and fro in a frenetic quest for meaning. A progressive orthodox church is an evangelical church, unwilling and even unable to keep the good news to itself, always ready to testify to the impact that knowing Jesus can have on the world.

Finally, the orthodox turn need not make us less progressive or less open to doubts and questions; instead we see ourselves as part of broader and deeper conversation, open to more perspectives, some of which will challenge our own. This is a healthy antidote to the narrow-mindedness that can develop in even the most liberal or inclusive settings. Living in a world of many stories requires of us that we be humble and ecumenical, delighting in what we might learn of God through the stories others share even as we delight in sharing the gift that has been entrusted to us.

Most of our congregations—if Ewart's analysis is to be believed—face extinction. Many of us have arrived at the place where we have nothing to lose by making a course correction and trying a different approach. The secular turn hasn't saved us. Maybe it is time we took a chance on the gospel and offered something more than baked goods, more than friendship even—an invitation into fellowship with Jesus Christ and his way of dying and rising and living in the kingdom, an invitation into a life that transcends the immanent frame and helps us to see the truth about the world; and an invitation into a relationship which promises that beyond the security for which we grasp lies the embrace of the One who reaches toward us in compassion and mercy.

# Conclusion

In a culture that has lost much of its Christian memory, re-Christianizing those affiliated with it may require as bold a venture as church union once seemed, with even more uncertainty about the outcome. Will its commitment to inclusion leave it with enough distinctiveness to thrive in a culture of diversity? . . . Will there be enough people on a spiritual quest for meaning, guidance, and consolation who want to belong to an organized community of faith? Will sufficient memory of its past survive to sustain its renewal in either a post-Christian or post-secular future?

—Phyllis D. Airhart, *A Church With the Soul of a Nation*[1]

A church that no longer asks about its theological foundations will be absorbed, sooner or later, into the general secular *melange*. It is only a matter of time.

—Douglas John Hall, *What Christianity Is Not*[2]

Phyllis D. Airhart concludes her recent history of the first forty years of the United Church of Canada with a series of questions about the future of the denomination. Wisely, in my opinion, she offers only a terse response to these richly nuanced questions: "Time will tell." The history

---

1. Airhart, *Church with the Soul of a Nation*, 299–300.
2. Hall, *What Christianity Is Not*, 109.

recounted in these pages affirms the wisdom of refraining from making too certain claims about the future, offering overly confident predictions based on current trends and trajectories. Secular theologians and their popularizers in the 1960s were confident they were witnessing the end of religion as it had been known to that point in history. They invited the church to exit its buildings and join the world, to flee from doctrine and dogma, creeds and practices, as though from a house on fire. The only things the church would need in this bold new age would be general principles distilled from the teachings of the somewhat exceptional man Jesus. In many respects the United Church of Canada of that time embraced this message, and it has continued to echo down across the decades, informing and inspiring new expressions of ecclesiology in the denomination.

But history did not turn out the way that secularists had imagined. The world today is in many respects a more religious place than it was then. Religion has reemerged as a powerful social force in many contexts around the globe, including in Canada. The standard secularization thesis, which read history in a linear fashion and predicted religion's extinction, turned out to be false—or at least, not so simple. Charles Taylor's revision or correction of the standard secularization thesis reintroduces complexity into the narrative and offers a more nuanced read of what we have witnessed over the past half century. Taylor's thesis invites us to reimagine *how* to be religious in a secular age. I have argued that a necessary ingredient in our search for a United Church response to Taylor's invitation is a commitment to the story at the heart of our tradition: the story of the life, death, and resurrection of Jesus Christ. Without a commitment to this story, we will, as Douglas John Hall predicts, "be absorbed . . . into the general secular melange." To some extent, this is already happening—it is surely at least a partial explanation of the United Church of Canada's decline in recent decades. Whether such an attempt to "re-Christianize" those currently affiliated with the United Church will succeed, whether it is possible to disciple those who have forgotten our story, or whether the future of the denomination will rely on reaching those currently outside its fellowship with the distinctive story of our tradition, only time will tell.

Still, I am convinced that we must try. We must offer, within the parameters of our particular branch of the Christian family tree, a portal to the riches of our tradition and a window open to transcendence, a view that draws us beyond the constraints of the immanent frame. William H. Willimon reminds us of what is at stake:

## CONCLUSION

So we must gather, on a regular basis, for worship. To speak about God in a world that lives as if there is no God. We must speak to one another as beloved brothers and sisters in a world which encourages us to live as strangers. We must pray to God to give us what we cannot have by our own efforts in a world which teaches us that we are self-sufficient and all-powerful. In such a world, what we do here on Sunday morning becomes a matter of life and death.[3]

Our world—the world God loves—needs us to offer our story, this treasure entrusted to us, this story the world otherwise would not know. Our story may seem simple and unsophisticated; it may not measure up to the fashions and standards of our day. We may even be embarrassed by its lack of consideration for the categories of modern philosophy and science. Yet, by the grace of God, this strange old story is the very thing our world needs.

---

3. Hauerwas and Willimon, *Resident Aliens*, 154.

# Author Biography

Jeff Seaton is an ordained minister in the United Church of Canada. Jeff earned a Master of Divinity from the Vancouver School of Theology in 2007, and was ordained to the ministry in May 2007. Following ordination, he was settled to the Kimberley pastoral charge in the shadow of the Rocky Mountains. In 2011, Jeff was called to serve the people of Trinity United Church in Vernon, British Columbia. He has served as chair of the British Columbia Conference Pastoral Relations Committee and as a member of the Conference Executive. Jeff earned a Doctor of Ministry from Duke University in 2016.

# Bibliography

Airhart, Phyllis D. *A Church with the Soul of a Nation: Making and Remaking the United Church of Canada*. Montreal & Kingston: McGill-Queen's University Press, 2014.
———. *Making and Remaking the United Church of Canada—Then and Now*. Webinar presented by the United Church of Canada, February 29, 2016.
Bagnell, Kenneth. "Secular Shift." *United Church Observer*, January 2011. http://www.ucobserver.org/faith/2011/01/secular_shift/.
Bass, Diana Butler. *Christianity After Religion: The End of Church and the Birth of a New Spiritual Awakening*. New York: HarperCollins, 2012.
Beardsall, Sandra. "Ray Hord: 'Prophet Evangelist' of the United Church." *Touchstone* 24 (September 2006) 48–59.
Berton, Pierre. *The Comfortable Pew: A Critical Look at Christianity and the Religious Establishment in the New Age*. Toronto: McLelland and Stewart, 1965.
Best, Marion. *Will Our Church Disappear: Strategies for the Renewal of the United Church of Canada*. Winfield, BC: Wood Lake, 1994.
Bibby, Reginald W. *A New Day: The Resilience and Restructuring of Religion in Canada*. Lethbridge: Project Canada, 2012.
Board of Evangelism and Social Service of the United Church of Canada. *Listen to the World: 40th Annual Report, 1965*. Toronto: United Church Publishing House, 1965.
———. *Why the Sea Is Boiling Hot: A Symposium on the Church and the World*. Toronto: Ryerson, 1965.
Boesveld, Sarah. "Sacred, Yes. But Is It Church?" *United Church Observer*, February 2011. http://www.ucobserver.org/faith/2011/02/sacred_church/.
Bokma, Anne. "In Church, Sort Of: Why Non-Believers Still Come on Sunday." Spiritual But Secular. *United Church Observer*, May 2016.
Bott, Richard. "Preliminary Report on the 'UCCan Ministers and god/God Survey.'" http://richardbott.com/download/uccan-ministers-and-god-survey-preliminary-report/.
Byassee, Jason. "Vancouver's Stony Soil: The Church in the Secular City." *Christian Century*, January 6, 2016.
Collins, Jim. *Good to Great: Why Some Companies Make the Leap . . . and Others Don't*. New York: HarperCollins, 2001.
Colorado, Carlos. "A Secular Age." *Touchstone* 28 (May 2010) 56–68.
Copenhaver, Martin B., Anthony B. Robinson, and William H. Willimon. *Good News in Exile: Three Pastors Offer a Hopeful Vision for the Church*. Grand Rapids: Eerdmans, 1999.
Cox, Harvey. *The Future of Faith*. New York: HarperCollins, 2009.

## BIBLIOGRAPHY

———. *The Secular City: Secularization and Urbanization in Theological Perspective.* Princeton: Princeton University Press, 2013.

Douglas, Scott. *Maybe One? A Theatrical History of the United Church,* 90th Anniversary Edition. Manuscript provided by the author.

Ewart, David. "Welcome to the Last Days of the United Church of Canada." http://www.davidewart.ca/United-Church-People-Trends-Projected-Based-on-2013.pdf.

———. "What Happened in 1965?" http://www.davidewart.ca/What-Happened-in-1965.pdf.

Faulkner, Tom. "With or Without God: Why the Way We Live is More Important Than What We Believe." *Touchstone* 27 (January 2009) 46–54.

Flatt, Kevin N. *After Evangelicalism: The Sixties and the United Church of Canada.* Montreal & Kingston: McGill-Queen's University Press, 2013.

Fletcher, Wendy. "Bonhoeffer: A Post-Colonial Ecclesiology for the Canadian Context." *Touchstone* 31 (February 2013) 14–26.

Frederic, Harold. *The Damnation of Theron Ware.* New York: Penguin, 1986.

Freed, Foster. "A Case for Liberal Evangelicalism." *Touchstone* 11 (January 1993) 33–44.

Gibbs, Eddie. *The Rebirth of the Church: Applying Paul's Vision for Ministry in Our Post-Christian World.* Grand Rapids: Baker Academic, 2013.

Goodwin, Douglas. "The Future of the Church." *Touchstone* 22 (September 2004) 15–21.

Grant, John Webster. *The Church in the Canadian Era.* Vancouver: Regent College Publishing, 1988.

———. "Unauthoritative Reflections on the United Church's Story." *Touchstone* 12 (January 1994) 4–12.

Grenz, Stanley J. "The Gospel and the Contemporary Pursuit of Spirituality." *Touchstone* 12 (May 1994) 32–36.

Hall, Douglas John. *What Christianity Is Not: An Exercise in 'Negative' Theology.* Eugene, OR: Cascade, 2013.

Harland, Gordon. "Religion, Canadian Style." *Touchstone* 10 (January 1992) 9–14.

Hart, David B. *Atheist Delusions: The Christian Revolution and Its Fashionable Enemies.* New Haven: Yale University Press, 2009.

———. "Christ and Nothing." *First Things* 136 (October 2003) 47–56. http://www.firstthings.com/article/2003/10/christ-and-nothing.

Haughton, William. "'A New Creed': Its Origins and Significance." *Touchstone* 29 (September 2011) 20–29.

Hauerwas, Stanley, and William H. Willimon. *Resident Aliens: Life in the Christian Colony.* Exp. 25th anniversary ed. Nashville: Abingdon, 2014.

Keller, Timothy, and John D. Inazu. "How Christians Can Bear Witness in an Anxious Age." *Christianity Today,* June 2016, web-only. http://www.christianitytoday.com/ct/2016/june-web-only/tim-keller-john-inazu-christians-gospel-witness-anxious-age.html.

Kilbourn, William, ed. *The Restless Church: A Response to the Comfortable Pew.* Toronto: McClelland and Stewart, 1966.

MacLean, Catherine Faith, and John H. Young. *Preaching the Big Questions: Doctrine Isn't Dusty.* Toronto: United Church Publishing House, 2015.

Manson, Ian M. "Re-Imagining the Church: Douglas John Hall and the Future of North American Christianity." *Touchstone* 15 (May 1997) 29–39.

McGrath, Alister E. "A Church Without Doctrine." *Touchstone* 10 (January 1992) 15–21.

Miedema, Gary. *For Canada's Sake: Public Religion, Centennial Celebrations, and the Remaking of Canada in the 1960s*. McGill-Queen's Studies in the History of Religion 2. Montreal: McGill-Queen's University Press, 2005.

Martin, David. *On Secularization: Towards a Revised General Theory*. Aldershot, UK: Ashgate, 2005.

Niebuhr, H. Richard. *Christ and Culture*. Exp. 50th anniversary ed. New York: HarperCollins, 2001.

Nietzsche, Friedrich. *Twilight of the Idols and the Anti-Christ*. Translated by R. J. Hollingdale. London: Penguin, 2003.

Noll, Mark. *What Happened to Christian Canada?* Vancouver: Regent College Publishing, 2007.

O'Toole, Roger, et al. "The United Church in Crisis: A Sociological Perspective on the Dilemmas of a Mainstream Denomination." *Studies in Religion/Sciences Religieuses* 20 (June 1991) 151–63.

Pentland, John. *Fishing Tips: How Curiosity Transformed a Community of Faith*. Toronto: Edge Network, 2015.

———. "Fishing Tips." Webinar presented by Edge: A Network for Ministry Development, the United Church of Canada, February 22, 2016.

———. Keynote Address, Holy Shift: Spirit Rising conference presented by BC Conference and Kamloops-Okanagan Presbytery of the United Church of Canada, Vernon, BC, April 22–24, 2016.

Robinson, John A. T. *Honest to God*. 40th anniversary ed. Louisville: Westminster John Knox, 2002.

Sayers, Mark. *Disappearing Church: From Cultural Relevance to Gospel Resilience*. Chicago: Moody, 2016.

Schweitzer, Don. "The Christology of John Dominic Crossan—And an Alternative." *Touchstone* 30 (January 2012) 25–34.

———, ed. *The United Church of Canada: A History*. Waterloo: Wilfrid Laurier University Press, 2012.

Searcy, Edwin. "Making Progress?" *Touchstone* 30 (January 2012) 7–14.

———. "The Story of My Conversion." *Touchstone* 27 (January 2009) 36–38. http://touchstonecanada.ca/wp-content/uploads/2013/08/Jan-2009-Heart.pdf.

Smith, James K. A. *How (Not) to Be Secular: Reading Charles Taylor*. Grand Rapids: Eerdmans, 2014.

Taylor, Charles. *A Secular Age*. Cambridge: Belknap Press of Harvard University Press, 2007.

Todd, Douglas. "Five Ways to Revive Liberal Religion." Vancouver Sun, September 11, 2015. http://blogs.vancouversun.com/2015/09/11/five-ways-to-revive-liberal-religion/.

Toronto Conference Interview Committee. "Report of Conference Interview Committee of Its Review of the Ministry of the Rev. Gretta Vosper." September 7, 2016. https://torontoconference.ca/wp-content/uploads/2016/09/Report-September-7-2016.pdf.

United Church of Canada. *The Manual, 2016*. Toronto: United Church Publishing House, 2016.

———. *Our Words of Faith*. Toronto: United Church of Canada, 2012.

———. *Year Book and Directory*. Toronto: United Church of Canada General Council Office, (various years).

## BIBLIOGRAPHY

United Church Observer Staff. "Beyond Belief." *United Church Observer*, October 2013. http://www.ucobserver.org/features/2013/10/beyond_belief/.

University Hill Congregation Ministry Profile and Search Committee. "Ministry Profile and Search Report (BC 400 MPSR) for Congregational Minister, University Hill Congregation," December 2015. http://uhill.net/docs/U%20Hill%20-%20Profile%20&%20Search%20-%20December%202015-1.pdf.

Vosper, Gretta. *Amen: What Prayer Can Mean In a World Beyond Belief.* Toronto: HarperCollins, 2013.

———. "A Little Bit About Me." grettavosper.ca, accessed August 15, 2016, http://www.grettavosper.ca/about/little-bit.

———. "My Answers to the Questions of Ordination." *Gretta Vosper: Minister, Author, Atheist* (blog), June 30, 2016. http://www.grettavosper.ca/answers-questions-ordination/.

———. *With or Without God: Why the Way We Live Is More Important Than What We Believe.* Toronto: HarperCollins, 2008.

Warner, Michael, Jonathan VanAntwerpen, and Craig Calhoun, eds. *Varieties of Secularism in a Secular Age.* Cambridge: Harvard University Press, 2013.

Wishart, Vernon R. "Beyond the Gospel of Liberalism." *Touchstone* 11 (September 1993) 24–31.

Wooley, Pieta. "Young, Smart and Into Jesus." *United Church Observer*, September 2016. http://ucobserver.org/faith/2016/09/millennial_ministers/.

Wyatt, Peter. "The New Atheism." *Touchstone* 32 (October 2014) 20–29.

———. "Post-Theism and the 'Problem' of God." *Touchstone* 30 (January 2012) 15–24.

Young, John H. "Evangelism in the United Church of Canada: Charles Templeton to Emerging Spirit." *Touchstone* 27 (January 2009) 27–35. http://touchstonecanada.ca/wp-content/uploads/2013/08/Jan-2009-Article3.pdf.

———. "What We Say We Believe Makes a Difference: The Remits on Doctrine in the United Church." *Touchstone* 29 (September 2011) 10–19.

Young, Pamela Dickey. "Theme and Variations: The Social Gospel in a New Key." *Toronto Journal of Theology* 12 (September 1996) 285–90.